Life after Divorce

BOBBIE REED, Ph.D.

CONCORDIA®

PUBLISHING HOUSE

Copyright © 1993 Concordia Publishing House
3558 S. Jefferson Avenue, St. Louis, MO 63118-3968
Manufactured in the United States of America

Library of Congress Cataloging in Publication Data
Reed, Bobbie.
    Life after divorce / Bobbie Reed.
      p.   cm.
ISBN 0-570-04614-9
    1. Divorced adults—Life skills guides. 2. Divorced adults—Conduct of life. 3. Divorced adults—Religious life. I. Title. HQ814.R45   1993
306.89—dc20   93-13412
CIP

---

1 2 3 4 5 6 7 8 9 10   02 01 00 99 98 97 96 95 94 93

To Carol Bostrom and Don Pugh
who ministered to me gently and lovingly
when my life fell apart
because of a divorce

Contents

As You Begin
Divorce! What an Ugly Word!

"I want a divorce!"

Those are four of the ugliest words in the world—words no one wants to hear. Words most people never want to say. When I heard them, I was shocked. Christians don't get divorced, I thought. I was *hurt*. What was so wrong with me that someone would want me out of his life forever? I was *scared*. What would I do now? Who would I be if I were divorced? How could I cope with raising two sons? How, and where, would I live? Where could I hide from the embarrassment of being divorced?

My divorce happened in 1973. I was 27 years old, and I had been raised in a strict Christian home. Although no one had actually said it, I understood that divorce was unforgivable. It was something one didn't do, no matter what happened. I didn't want a divorce. I didn't want to be divorced. I felt *powerless* and *confused*. For weeks, I would fall asleep and dream of falling deep into an unknown space. Terrified, I would wake up attempting to scream for help, but only manage a soft croak. I would lie there, reminding myself that it was only a dream, my heart pounding loudly, my breathing rapid and labored. Night after night I tossed and turned; morning after morning I awoke, still tired. I just didn't know how to endure this rejection.

Divorce is hard. It is hard for the one who is left; it is hard for the person who leaves. Both suffer.

The person who "leaves " may feel driven out and rejected or may have tried single-handedly to make the marriage work and finally admitted failure. Usually the person who leaves has already mourned for the relationship. Long before deciding to leave, that person has suffered inside, often quietly—doing what was possible, grieving, and then giving up.

The person who remains usually feels rejected, hurt, angry, and scared. Even if he/she was aware of the problems, that person has not given up on the relationship. At the time of the divorce he/she must begin the mourning recovery. Not recognizing that the two former partners are in different steps of recovery the one who remains may comment bitterly that the other has no feelings, does not care, or is not suffering.

On rare occasions, one or both persons may experience a sense of relief. This does not mean that the divorce was easy. It may mean that the pain of the divorce and the grieving for the death of the marriage occurred while the couple was still technically married. The"emotional divorce" happened much earlier.

A few people stuff their feelings down so deeply that they are not aware that they are even in pain. But in these cases, the repressed hurt and grief will surface eventually, often long after the divorce experience. It is best to acknowledge the pain early and to begin working through grief to become whole again.

Two married persons form an identity as a couple that affects each person's individual identity. When the marriage is dissolved, the couple identity is destroyed, and the self-concept and self-esteem of the two usually suffer. They must take stock, redefine their personal identities, rebuild their individual lives, and in many ways, start a whole new life.

Relational psychologists tell us that it may take half as long as the relationship lasted to fully recover from its loss. Some say that a minimum of two-and-a-half to three-and-a-half years is required for complete healing. With therapy, counseling, or other appropriate action, that recovery time can be shortened significantly. Dr. Zev Wanderer, founder of the Center for Behavior Therapy in Beverly Hills, California, researched and perfected through years of field-testing an approach, which if followed, can virtually guarantee some relief within a 12-week period. This doesn't mean that a person will be totally free from memories, from residual sadness, or from the occasional setback, or that the person will be totally healed. It does mean that a person can work through most of the devastating initial pain, regain control over life, and become functional within 12 weeks.

This book combines the psychologically effective behavioral techniques suggested by Dr. Wanderer (in *Letting Go* by Dr. Zev Wanderer and Tracy Cabot, Dell, 1987) with experiences of fellow travelers who have journeyed through the valley of divorce, Scripture principles for hope and healing, and theologically sound affirmations to use daily to strengthen your resolve to become whole again. This approach was first explained in my book *Prescription for a Broken Heart* (Regal, 1982).

This book is written primarily for people who are in those early days of shock and pain. It is not intended to be read in one sitting. Instead, take a chapter a week. Read the material. Reread it. Be sure to do the suggested activities, even if they seem silly, ineffective, unnecessary, or too hard. Reflect on, and respond to, the questions at the end of the chapter. Use the affirmations daily. If, at the end of one week, you are not ready to move to the next chapter, stay on the same chapter for another week. However, don't spend more than two weeks on any one chapter, or your recovery will be delayed unnecessarily.

This book is also written for people who have been divorced awhile, but who find that they are not through with the grieving process, or that they have not yet regained control over their own lives. If you are in this group, start reading from the beginning of the book until you find the step where you are stuck in your recovery process. Start your application of the material at that chapter, or perhaps at the chapter immediately preceding it, as that may be where you are actually resisting recovery.

This book is also written for friends, counselors, or pastors of persons going through a divorce. It will help you understand what your friends are experiencing. It will provide you with ideas you can share with them, particularly if they are not the kind who read books such as this one and get help for themselves.

The normal grieving process involves several predictable stages: shock, denial, bargaining, depression, anger, acceptance, and hope.

I discovered through my own experiences that people do not always go through the recovery and rebuilding process in a straight line from devastation to wholeness. Progress is often two steps forward and one step back. Sometimes it is even one step forward and two steps back! But those who really want to get past the pain and begin to live again will find that they can do so, not only in their own strength, but with strength the Lord gives.

What a great God we love and serve! He does indeed hate divorce (Mal. 2:16), but He loves us, unconditionally and forever (Jer. 31:3; Rom. 8:38–39). Nothing we could ever do, including being divorced, would be enough to separate us from that love. So in spite of what happens in our lives, we are free to come to Him asking for His forgiveness, His help, His comfort, and His guidance. Once again, the Gospel triumphs over the Law, and we experience God's greatness in terms of His grace and His love.

During the early days of the pain of a divorce, there will be a temptation to live by your feelings. This is not wise. Your feelings will fluctuate. One minute you may feel hopeful and serene; the next you may be hopelessly depressed. This is normal. Don't let this emotional roller coaster fool you into thinking that it will always be like this. It won't.

- In Christ, believe that you will survive this experience, for you will.
- In Christ, believe that you will take charge of your own life again, for you can.
- In Christ, believe that God is sovereign and will help you through, for He will.
- In Christ, stay strong in your faith, through study of God's Word and partaking of the Sacrament, for they will sustain you.
- In Christ, claim the promise: "Blessed are those who mourn, for they will be comforted" (Matt. 5:4), for He will comfort you.

It took a few years for Christ to help me through my own recovery. Oh, I rebuilt a life fairly quickly because I was a single mom with two little boys ages six and eight, and life had to go on. But inside my heart, the pain continued. I didn't know how to make the pain go away faster. Doing some right things— some, I'm sure, by divine intervention and some by applying suggestions from friends and good books—I eventually found the scars of the divorce were fading. I actually felt Christ's power helping me design and shape a new, and maybe better, life for me and my kids. I could live a broken existence, or I could live in—with God's help—wholeness. I celebrate the whole life God has given me. You will too.

1

"I Don't Want to Be Divorced!"

Your first response to the idea of a divorce was probably the same as mine: *I don't want to be divorced!* Rejection is always a shock. Even if your marriage has been deteriorating for a long time, it is still hard to face the fact that it will end in a divorce. Most of us hope that things will get better. We hope in spite of the reality of what is happening. We hope when it no longer makes sense to hope. And then, we secretly hope even when all hope is gone! We don't want to admit that our marriage has failed.

The one person you care most about in your life has just walked out. You feel that you have lost the only thing of value to you, a love relationship with your mate. You are in shock. You are numb. There is no strong emotional response because you are immobilized. The shock response actually provides a little of the emotional space and padding that you will need when you first face the possibility of a divorce. When Janine's husband told her he wanted a divorce, she looked at him blankly, then asked him what he wanted for supper that night. Nothing was registering because she was in shock. She couldn't understand or accept what was going on, so she rejected the idea.

The shock initally leads to denial that this is happening to you. You have a vague sense that if you just stand still, it won't happen. You can't take it all in. Your mind is rejecting the idea. This can't be happening, you tell yourself. It is all a cruel joke. This is just a temporary, crazy notion. He/she will be back. If you are in denial, you may fall into one or more of these behavior patterns:

- Perry tried to keep his life going as normally as possible. He did the laundry, cooked the meals, went to work, took care of the car, went out with friends, and never mentioned the fact that his spouse had moved out or discussed the possibility of divorce.
- Coral pulled away from her friends and her spouse, as well as her job, in an attempt to distance herself from people who might know what was going on. In that way, she could refuse to face the facts.
- Harold intensified his spiritual activities (reading the Bible, going to church, praying) to see if God would make his spouse abandon the idea of divorce.
- Jim filled his life with lots of new and different tasks to keep him from thinking about the idea of a divorce. Suddenly, he had the energy to complete all of the unfinished projects he had ignored for the last 10 years.
- Phyllis began spending time with her in-laws to reassure herself that the family configuration was not going to change.
- Oliver tried to bargain with his spouse to keep her from leaving. Suddenly, nothing was as important to him as keeping the marriage intact.

Denial Is Natural

As the initial shock wears off, it is natural to want to deny what is happening. It's too frightening to face the implications a divorce would have in your life.

Remember when you first fell in love? Wasn't it wonderful?

Being in romantic love is like having a magic mirror in which we always appear beautiful, handsome, talented, strong, and terrific. People in love temporarily lose touch with reality, as they begin to live a fantasy existence. Suddenly all of the love songs are unbelievably true. The sky is bluer. The birds do sing sweetly. Eyes sparkle. Cheeks flush. Tender glances speak volumes. Life becomes an adventure for two. And, since so much of the fairy tale notions about love seem to be coming true, then it must also follow that the *living happily ever after part* will be true.

As time passes, married couples realize that life together is not *always* wonderful; yet a part of us tries to hang onto the fairy tale. In the fairy tale there is no place for divorce. You may find that you are clinging to your spouse at this stage of the process, more from a reluctance to lose the fairy tale than because you don't want to live without that person. Uppermost in your mind is the question of how to get your loved one to return and to resume the marriage. You don't want another love, not even a better one. In fact, if you genuinely believe that there is no hope for a reconciliation, you might not even want to live.

But live you must! God is watching over you. Ps. 56:8 says that God catches your tears in a bottle and records them in His book. 1 Peter 5:7 tells us to cast all our cares on Him, because He loves us. Don't give up faith at this point. God will never give up on you.

Isn't There a Chance for Reconciliation?

"I believe that there is always a chance for a reconciliation," Anna says. *"If I didn't believe that, I think that I couldn't face another day."*

Yes, there is always a chance that you and your spouse will reconcile. There is a possibility that you can build a stronger marriage than you have ever had. There is also a possibility that it will not happen. But you wouldn't be human if you didn't have at least a few thoughts, fantasies, or hopes of reconciliation.

Part of denial is trying to do something—anything—to stop a divorce. As you think back over the marriage and remember the things you fought about, you decide that they just aren't that important if they are going to cost you your marriage. Your perspective is suddenly different! Who cares whether there are socks on the bedroom floor, toothpaste squeezed in the middle, or cabinet doors left open? Not you! You easily and eagerly resolve to change, to become a different person. You will do all of the things your spouse wanted you to do (shave off your beard, lose weight, clean and cook the fish he/she caught, or cut up the charge cards). You will abandon the annoying habits that annoyed your spouse. Magically, you will become magically more supportive, more loving, more affectionate, more sexual, and more understanding. It seems easy. Now that you know divorce is the alternative, you will just decide to be different. You can't wait to pick up the telephone and call your spouse to share the good news. A divorce is no longer necessary! You will "fix" things!

But it is not that easy.

Sometimes a temporary separation and subsequent reconciliation make relationships stronger, but there are some conditions for a successful reconciliation. Through the guidance and power of the Holy Spirit:

1. Both persons must want the reconciliation. One person can start the reconciliation process. Initally, one person may make more concessions, but in the long run, both persons must truly want to work at the reconciliation, or it will be short-lived at best.

Compare this with how we are reconciled with God. *He* wants a personal relationship with us. *He* provided the sacrifice of Christ on the cross. *He* offers forgiveness. *He* seals that reconciliation in our Baptism. His Holy Spirit gives us the power to live in a daily relationship with Him, strengthening it through reading His Word, through prayer, and through receiving the Lord's Supper. Look at John 1:11–13. Jesus came to establish a relationship with His people; we respond to His great love. The same is true today in our relationship with the Lord and in our relationship with one another. Relationships are two-way.

2. Both persons must recognize that what they almost lost is valuable to them. A reconciliation doesn't work if one person simply agrees to come back *for the other person's sake.* Both must see the relationship as precious.

3. Both persons must put time and energy into the relationship. Just agreeing to reconcile and moving back together won't make the marriage work. Both persons need to be honest about what did not work in the relationship and what needs to be changed. Both must be willing to listen and to say what they agree to work on. This is the same in our relationship with God. Matt. 6:33 tells us to give priority to our relationship with Him ("seeking the kingdom") before we focus on other things.

4. Both persons must confess their failures to one another, forgive, and accept forgiveness. Reconciliation will not work if past mistakes, failures, cruelties, and thoughtlessness remain unacknowledged, unforgiven and rehashed. Look to God's own example in Ps. 103:8–12. In His steadfast love, He removes our transgressions "as far as the east is from the west."

5. Both persons must agree to work on rebuilding trust. Trust is earned, but the process can be expedited if both persons agree to start out fresh, believing in each other rather than expecting failure.

6. Both persons must agree to put Christ in the center of their lives and their marriage. When the primary focus of relationship is on human beings, there can only be problems. Humans are not perfect; they will let one another down. When relationships are built on Christ, there is a chance for success, because He will never let us down. If we are focusing on Christ, we can tolerate human failings more easily.

Eph. 5:21–33 gives the relationship of Christ and the church as the model for total love and commitment of a husband and wife.

7. Both persons must be willing to give the reconciliation time to work. One cannot successfully "reconcile" for a few days to see if it will work. It won't. A marriage that took years to fall apart cannot be put back together in a few days. A decision to reconcile requires a commitment of a few months—and ultimately a lifetime.

8. Both persons must be willing to seek professional assistance with the reconciliation. A neutral, third party can provide insight and diffuse the strong emotions that exist between the two persons striving for a reconciliation. A Christian counselor who can combine biblical principles with psychological assistance can be invaluable in your reconciliation.

Note that the first two words of each of these conditions is *both persons*. If only one person wants to attempt a reconciliation, it probably won't work. A healthy relationship is one in which both persons learn to give and take. If only one person wants to get back together, it is okay to try, but the chances of success are slim.

Proceed Prayerfully

If you and your partner agree to reconcile, proceed prayerfully. Before your first meeting spend a quiet evening—or several—with God. Read His Word. Read Ps. 139:23–24 and pray those verses David wrote. Ask the Holy Spirit to search your own heart and reveal where you need to grow and develop in order to be a better partner. Write down those things that He brings to your mind. Commit yourself to approach your partner in a Christ-like and forgiving spirit rather than from a hurt, resentful, or judgmental position.

Be careful not to confuse a temporary feeling of expansive generosity—a "what's done is done" attitude—toward your beloved with true forgiveness. Neither is forgiveness a desperate bargaining position of "nothing else matters if you will come back to me." Instead, true forgiveness comes from God, who will give you the ability to say, "I have forgiven the past just as God, for Christ's sake, has forgiven me. I will no longer hold it against you."

The generosity or bargaining approaches are emotional acts; genuine forgiveness is a rational commitment. Ask God to prepare the heart of the one you love so there will be a receptiveness to your actions of reconciliation. Ask for guidance and wisdom as you plan how to work together toward a renewed marriage.

Start Over

Now that you have agreed to start over, the hard work begins. Obviously, there must be changes on both sides. If there are no changes, the reconciliation won't last. The old relationship did not work. The "new" relationship must be just that—a *new relationship!* You will want to build a new marriage that salvages all of the good from the previous relationship, but which discards all that did not work.

Identify what needs to be worked on. Each of you make three lists:

- Behaviors that enhanced our prior relationship
- Behaviors that detracted from our old relationship
- Behaviors that can strengthen our future relationship

The first list highlights the positive aspects of the old relationship and affirms each of you. It might include such things as the following:

- Your cooking attractive meals
- Our spending Thursday nights going out together
- Your remembering my birthday and holidays with special cards
- Your complimenting my appearance
- My listening when you share about work-related problems
- My doing yard work
- Your support when I lost my job

The second list identifies actions (usually of the other person) that are irritating or hurtful. It is basically a list of grievances. (Remember that you have made a commitment to God that the past is forgiven, so list behaviors that may cause problems in the relationship in the future, and don't bring up one-time offenses from the past!) Things on the second list might include the following:

- Your spending too much time on the telephone with your friends
- Your bringing home a lot of work from the job every day
- Your spending every leisure hour in front of the television
- Your being so jealous I can't talk to another woman/man

The third list tends to be those behaviors that you want substituted for those on the second list. For example:

- Your spending at least one hour alone with me each day
- Your waiting until after dinner to discuss problems you had during the day
- Your being on time
- Your giving me at least one compliment a day

When you have completed your lists, discuss what you have written. Share how you felt when the things on the first two lists occurred. Tell how you think you would feel if the things on the third list were to occur. Together decide on which things you will work on together and in which order. Keep the conversation positive and do not let it become an argument. Pray together, making your commitment not only a promise to each other but a vow to God.

Building your new relationship into a strong and healthy union will require a daily commitment and a lot of work, but the results are worth it.

Sometimes Reconciliation Doesn't Work

Michele and Ray were halfway through the divorce process when they began to realize that they still loved each other enough to give their marriage one more try. They met and talked honestly about what was wrong with their relationship. They went to a counselor. They spent time getting to know one another in different ways than they had during the marriage. They practiced new ways of relating. They gave the reconciliation process more than a year, but in the end they still decided to be divorced. They could not achieve a total commitment to one another.

Perhaps you give the reconciliation effort everything you can, but it just doesn't work. Your spouse leaves again. Once again, you face the fact that divorce possibly will be a reality. You may wonder if it was worth all your efforts to rebuild the marriage.

Trying to reconcile is always worth the effort, because you will always know that you did everything you could to make the marriage work. Also, you will gain more closure on the past because through the reconciliation process you have worked through some issues in the relationship. You have committed to forgiving your spouse for past and present failures. (Don't go back on that decision.) And you have accepted the fact that some of your behavior in relationships needs to change if you are to succeed in future relationships. These steps will bring you closer to the reality that your marriage is over and you must move ahead.

The period of denial is over. You are moving through the grieving process.

I Want to Talk about It!

At this step you may find that you want to talk about what is happening. You want to talk to anyone, friends, co-workers, family members, strangers on the street! You want to cry out at the injustice of what is happening.

This is not wise at this time.

If you do talk, you will receive conflicting responses. Some will say you are better off without your spouse. Some will be shocked; they had no idea your marriage was in trouble. Some will blame you for not being a better spouse. Some will shrug at your pain and tell you to forget your spouse and get a new love right away. Some will tell you the story of their own divorces. A few will tell you they saw it coming and are surprised that you didn't.

You don't need to hear all of this right now. So, wait awhile before you start talking. This doesn't mean that you can't talk at all.

1. Talk to God. God is listening. Come to Him with everything. Tell Him exactly how you are feeling and what you are thinking. (He already knows, so you don't need to hide anything.) Peter tells us to cast all our concerns and anxieties on God, for He cares what happens in our lives (1 Peter 5:7).

2. Talk to one or two persons you can trust. You can talk to a counselor, a pastor, or trusted friend. Solomon advocated having trusted counselors. Without good advice, we would all be in trouble (Prov. 11:14; 15:22).

3. Write your thoughts. Start a journal or diary. Pour out your feelings and thoughts on paper. Even if you repeat yourself, that's okay. Just let the words flow until you feel relief from your compulsion to talk.

4. Have short, imaginary conversations with your spouse. Visualize your spouse sitting in a chair and have short, imaginary conversations where you can say what you are feeling. Talk out loud, speak with feeling—just as if that person were actually listening. Get all of those thoughts and feelings out until you experience relief.

5. Share in small groups at a divorce recovery support group program. If you attend a divorce recovery support group program, you can feel free to share with other people who are going through their own divorce experience. Sharing in this context will help you gain perspective as you hear the stories of others.

After a separation the first week or so will be the hardest. The emotional trauma will keep your stomach churned and your thoughts spinning. But it will get better. Just take life one day at a time, one step at a time, and one prayer at a time.

Use Affirmations

Each chapter will give you one or more affirmations to use as you move through the grieving process and begin rebuilding your life. The affirmations provided will state a fact or a decision of importance to your recovery and personal growth. Each affirmation has several accompanying Scripture verses upon which it is based. Here's how to use the affirmations.

Copy the affirmations and the Scriptures on 3×5 cards.

Pray for God's guidance. Then read and repeat the affirmations aloud five times, at least five different times each day:

- When you get up in the morning
- Mid-morning (on your coffee break at work)
- At lunchtime
- Mid-afternoon (on your break at work)

- Before bed

Say the affirmations firmly, with conviction. Jesus has already won our victory over sin so you can repeat the affirmations believing that God can make them come true in your life. Ask Him to do so. Claim the promise of Matt. 21:22, which states that if you ask anything *believingly,* in Christ's name, it will be granted to you.

Read the accompanying Scripture referencess at least once five times a day.

Continue repeating previous affirmations as new ones are added each week. It won't take much time to repeat 12 to 15 affirmations once you have learned them well.

Here is the affirmation for this chapter:

Affirmation of Faith

"My faith in God is strong, because it is based on the Word of God. I feel confident because of my strong faith."

Heb. 11:1: "Now faith is being sure of what we hope for and certain of what we do not see."

Rom. 10:17: "Consequently, faith comes from hearing the message, and the message is heard through the word of Christ."

Rom. 5:1: "Therefore, since we have been justified through faith, we have peace with God through our Lord Jesus Christ."

Gal. 3:2, 5: "I would like to learn just one thing from you: Did you receive the Spirit by observing the law, or by believing what you heard? . . . Does God give you His Spirit and work miracles among you because you observe the law, or because you believe what you heard?"

Reflections

At the end of each chapter, a "reflections" section will help you respond to the ideas in the text. Be honest with yourself as you spend a few minutes responding to each question.

These questions also are a good activity for a divorce recovery support group.

Still, the best alternative is to start a personal journal during your divorce recovery. Use it to record your thoughts and feelings, your prayers, verses you find helpful during this time, *and* your responses to the reflection questions.

Reflections

- How did you feel when you were first confronted with the reality that your marriage was ending in a divorce?
- What did you tell yourself?
- In what ways did you act as if it weren't happening?
- What attempts did you make at reconciliation?
- What happened?
- What good came from the attempts at reconciliation?
- How was your faith in God affected (either strengthened or weakened) by the separation and divorce?
- Where are you spiritually today?
- In what ways has your prayer life changed since the issue of divorce was raised?
- What are you doing right now to cope with what is happening in your marriage and in your life?

Coping Activities

Check off the following activities given in this chapter, as you complete them:

- [ ] 1. Tell God what you are thinking and feeling.
- [ ] 2. Start a personal journal.
- [ ] 3. Talk with a counselor, pastor, or friend.
- [ ] 4. Hold short, imaginary conversations with your spouse.
- [ ] 5. Attend a divorce recovery support group.
- [ ] 6. Use the affirmations.

2

"I Feel So Depressed"

Carla was depressed. She had finally acknowledged to herself that her husband was not coming back and that she was single again. She looked around her home and her life, feeling that everything was wrong and there was no one to help put things right. She went into a serious depression that lasted several weeks.

You feel devastated and depressed. The one you loved so much is gone and isn't coming back. Your attempts to reconcile have failed, and the romantic relationship is really over. Perhaps your divorce is final, or your spouse has found someone new to love. When you think of a future without the one you loved so much, it doesn't seem worth the living. Don't be surprised by the intensity of these feelings; they are normal.

Not only has your spouse left, but with him/her also went the fantasy of love that would last forever, the primary source of love in your life, the adventure, the sparkle, and the hope. Only a romantic partner can keep the fantasy of romantic love alive, causing partners to form dependencies that require contact and interaction with one another. It is like an addiction. When one partner leaves, the other is deprived of the primary source of love, and there is a strong, almost irresistible, urge to contact the other for a "love fix." There can be actual, physical pain as the body goes through the withdrawal of love support. You may experience stomach cramps, ulcer flare-ups, muscle spasms, headaches, or other stress-related symptoms.

If you want to read a Bible passage with which you might identify, read Jeremiah's song of woe (Lam. 3:1–20). What an excellent description of how it feels to be so depressed and sad that you experience physical symptoms of pain and discomfort!

Your withdrawal may include any number of other behaviors that may make you think you are going crazy. You may not be able to concentrate on any task, think that you are going insane, feel that you are a total failure, experience insomnia, lose your appetite, spend an inordinate amount of time trying to plan how to get your spouse back, or neglect your job, self, children, or friends. Don't worry—as unsettling as such behaviors are—they are typical, and they won't last forever.

Evaluate your behaviors against the following lists. If you experience most of these behaviors every day, consider professional assistance to get you through this step of the healing process. But don't be concerned that you are losing your mind when you find yourself doing many of these things at first. It is normal to go a little crazy in the aftermath of losing a love.

Obsessive behaviors:

- Can't concentrate
- Watching the telephone, waiting for your spouse to call
- Deliberately listening to sad music
- "Seeing" your spouse everywhere you go
- Spending long hours in imaginary conversation with your spouse
- Thinking about committing yourself to a psychiatric institution
- Thinking of ways to make your spouse suffer

Compulsive behaviors:

- Following strangers because you are sure they are your spouse
- Telling your story to anyone who will listen
- Starting to overdose on junk foods or alcohol
- Starting to smoke
- Driving by your spouse's house or office
- Telephoning your spouse repeatedly
- Keeping your spouse's favorite foods in the house for "when he/she returns"

Depressive behaviors:

- Sleeping excessively and withdrawing from all outside activities and friends
- Blaming yourself for everything that went wrong in the marriage
- Neglecting yourself, car, children, pets, garden, house, yard, bills, friends, or job
- Crying excessively
- Thinking you are helpless, hopeless, a failure, unlovable, ugly, or unable to cope
- Giving away prized personal possessions
- Thinking about, planning, or even attempting suicide

Phobic behaviors:

- Feeling the world is closing in on you
- Panicking when confronted with new situations or people
- Turning on all the lights and the television to push away the loneliness
- Suddenly being afraid of growing old, of losing your looks, of being unable to support yourself
- Wanting to run away
- Avoiding places you and your spouse used to go
- Being unable to be alone

Psychosomatic behaviors:

- Frequent headaches, nausea, heartburn, diarrhea, or chest pains
- Rapid heartbeat
- Frequent shortness of breath or hyperventilation
- Physical illnesses such as colds, flu, allergy attacks, or rashes
- Muscle spasms
- Being unable to sleep well
- Sudden intolerances to certain foods

Hysterical behaviors:

- Becoming highly irritated at almost anything
- Panicking frequently
- Forgetting important tasks, dates, and commitments
- Losing your temper constantly
- Being unable to tolerate noise or silence
- Becoming careless and having "accidents"
- Feeling that you would give anything, do anything, or promise anything to get your spouse back

The lists help you see that unusual and nonproductive behaviors are common after losing a spouse. These behaviors are not helpful in the healing process, but once you recognize them you are more able to take charge of your life and get through the grieving.

Even when sad and depressed we need to remember God's power and faithfulness. Read Ps. 38:1–22 and see how David prayed to God when he was feeling down.

Paraphrased, he said, "I can't rest. My wounds stink! I am troubled and bowed down. I mourn all day long. I feel sick. I am weak and I groan with pain. I can't see ahead. My lovers and friends have left me. People are out to get me and hurt me, and they say bad things about me."

Sound familiar?

Then David reminds himself that God hears his prayers and will not forsake or leave him. God is always ready to hear and help you and me also.

But I Wish I Were Dead!

As you think of the future without your spouse, perhaps you can't see yourself living at all. This is normal. Most people, even Christians, have fleeting thoughts of suicide after the loss of a love relationship. Just remember that ending your life is not the answer to your pain.

When I was at this stage of my grieving process, I didn't think of suicide as an act of getting even with my former spouse or even as self-murder. I just wanted relief from the incredible pain I was experiencing. I just wanted it to be over.

But the Holy Spirit kept bringing Bible verses to my mind to keep me going one day at a time.

- Is. 43:2: "When you pass through the waters, I will be with you; and when you pass through the rivers, they will not sweep over you. When you walk through the fire, you will not be burned; the flames will not set you ablaze."

- Ps. 23:4: "Even though I walk through the valley of the shadow of death, I will fear no evil, for You are with me; Your rod and Your staff, they comfort me."

The Holy Spirit would remind me that Jesus Christ understood what I was going through. (See Heb. 4:14–16.) In Luke 22—23 I discovered that He was rejected several times. He was betrayed by one friend, rejected by another, beaten and mocked by strangers, ignored by religious leaders, crucified between two criminals, jeered by the crowd, and deserted by friends, family, and acquaintances. I read David's words in Psalm 22 that described Jesus' feelings as He hung on the cross and even had the Father turn away from Him. I could see that my Lord did, indeed, understand how I felt.

Being able to come to my Lord in prayer and pour out the hurt—knowing that He had been there—helped me through those early, dark days.

Stay Alive

If you have frequent thoughts or strong urges toward ending your life, you need to take immediate steps.

1. Make it hard to take your own life. Most people who contemplate suicide have a preferred scenario for the act. Take steps to put the means outside of your control for following through with your scenario. Depending upon your fantasy,

- flush poisons, drugs, sleeping pills, or tranquilizers down the toilet;
- give your straight razor blades, sharp knives, and guns to a friend who will promise not to let you have them back for several weeks;
- stay away from cliffs, roofs, and top floors of tall buildings;
- avoid driving alone by car pooling or taking the bus to work;
- have the gas turned off in your home;
- don't go to the ocean, to the river, or swim alone;
- avoid walking across bridges.

2. Keep emergency phone numbers near your telephone. Your list should include family members, your pastor, three or four close friends, your counselor, your local crisis line, and even the police. Confess your thoughts of suicide to your family and friends. Commit to calling one or more of them when the urges get strong.

3. Avoid being alone during the time of the day when your urge or compulsion for suicide is usually strong. Visit a friend, go to a movie, have a friend stay over with you, go to a singles function, go shopping at an all-night grocery store, go to an all-night restaurant for a bowl of soup. Do something to be with other people.

You don't have to want to be with anyone or to do what you are doing. Your purpose is not to enjoy yourself, but to stay alive.

Cope with the Pain

When we experience a deep, personal loss, we face the grieving and recovery process. This process includes several steps: shock, denial, bargaining, depression, anger, forgiveness, acceptance, hope, and joy. In the early days after a loss, the concept of joy seems unrealistic and even undesirable. With divorce, we can't have the one we love, so we don't want to be happy. The idea is preposterous! Don't worry about the last steps of the process right now. Concentrate on where you are today.

After surviving the shock, denial, and bargaining to try to get your spouse back, you begin to acknowledge privately that your spouse has truly left. You are alone. And you will tend to intensify that aloneness by withdrawing from the other parts of your life.

You are depressed.

You think about your loss all the time. You notice the sad songs on the radio and identify with the words of each one. Since the person you loved most has withdrawn love, you tell yourself you're unlovable and will never be loved again. You can remember every little thing you did wrong in the relationship, and you feel an inordinate amount of guilt. You secretly believe that you are the cause for the breakup and that you should have been a better spouse. You are listless and don't care about your appearance, your bills, your house, your children, or your friends. At work, you barely do enough to keep from being fired. You just don't care.

Perhaps in every way but the physical, you are actually committing suicide. For example:

- Are you *jeopardizing your health* through neglect or unnecessary risks?
- Are you *committing career suicide* by neglecting your job, failing to show up or being chronically tardy?
- Is your *social life dying* because you are cutting people off, failing to keep commitments, being obnoxious, or refusing to talk?
- Are you *emotionally atrophying* because you have decided to protect yourself from future pain by refusing to feel anything ever again?
- Are you choosing *psychological suicide* by assuming all the blame for the failed relationship by putting yourself down, harboring negative attitudes, giving into fear and depression, and by reinforcing a poor self-image?
- Have you *neglected your spiritual life* by not going to church, reading God's Word, praying, fellowshiping with other believers, and walking by faith?

People tend to respond to personal crises by drawing nearer to God or by withdrawing and blaming Him. In the depression stage of grieving, there is often a tendency to withdraw and blame. If this is where you are, decide not to give in. Instead, deliberately turn to God and spend time in prayer with Him.

Take Positive Action

When her husband left, Violet began fantasizing about suicide because she discovered that she didn't have any close friend to turn to. It seemed that everyone was merely a casual acquaintance. No one was with her during her journey through grief.

The idea of suicide may be attractive now because life has no meaning for you. The one person who provided a purpose for your life has left you, and now you are asking "why live?"

During your marriage, you may have neglected other relationships; discarded other sources of affirmation; or developed an unrealistic concept of your spouse.

You can take charge of these aspects of your life and reduce the attractiveness of suicide.

1. Rebuild neglected relationships. *Edna had built her life around her home and her husband. She had stopped writing to her high school friends. She no longer sang in the church choir. She gave up acting in the community theater. No wonder that she felt all alone and abandoned when she started through her divorce.*

In a marriage, we often focus most of our attention on our relationship with a spouse and neglect other important relationships. When our marriage ends, we turn to friends and discover that they are not waiting for us. They have gone on with their own lives.

Friendships from the marriage tend to be linked to the relationship with our spouses. So, looking to these people for support is not always positive. Friends of a couple usually feel that comforting or socializing with one partner is rejecting the other. Therefore, these friends tend to take sides with one partner or to withdraw from both to avoid taking sides at all.

You may not have been close to your family during the marriage.

So here you are, alone and lonely, needing friends, and unsure where to turn. Recognize that you may have to develop new friendships or rebuild old relationships. Call a couple of old friends. Go out for coffee or to a movie. Catch up on each other's lives. Write letters to friends who do not live in your city. Telephone cousins or family members with whom you used to have fun. Visit your family and do familiar things from long ago together—chop wood, bake cookies, look at old home movies, do spring cleaning.

When reconnecting, you don't have to discuss your divorce. In fact, you can make the topic off limits at first. Your primary purpose is to regain a connection with other human beings.

2. Take charge of the details of your life. *Doug's neighbors knew something was going wrong at his house. His newspapers stacked up on the driveway. Once neatly manicured, his lawn was unkept and ugly. Without watering, the grass began to die. Doug was not interested in the details. He had a bigger problem to focus on—his divorce.*

During the stages of shock, denial, and bargaining, you let several areas of your life go untended. Over a few weeks this neglect may create bigger problems than you can imagine! A neglected lawn is not noticeable the first two weeks, but later, you may have either a jungle or a desert surrounding your home. You can get by without doing the laundry for a couple of weeks, but then you are reduced to sorting through the hamper for your cleanest dirty shirt or blouse! You may leave the bills unpaid, your checkbook unbalanced, grocery shopping undone, and dishes unwashed. It's time to take charge— right now!

Even the thought of little tasks makes you tired, so the idea of regaining control of your life seems impossible. Don't try to do it all in one day! List things that you need to do and cross them off as you complete them. Start with the easy ones to get some momentum. Water the dying plants and toss out the dead ones. Clean the house. Hire someone to mow the lawn. Organize the laundry and start on it. Drop off the dry cleaning.

Do something each day. You don't have to accomplish miracles, but do accomplish something. And it is important to acknowledge your accomplishments, because they combat the powerlessness you are experiencing from having someone else decide that you are going to be divorced.

Notice and appreciate the order that you are bringing back into your life. You *do* have the power to structure your time and direct your energies. You are worth a tidy house, clean clothes, and a fully stocked kitchen.

List the chores your spouse used to do and decide how each one will be handled. If he changed the oil in the cars, will you learn to do this or have it done? Did she tend the lawn? Will you do it now, or will you hire it out? List telephone numbers you need for household emergencies—a mechanic, plumber, electrician, doctor, dentist, handyman, baby-sitter, and yard worker. Now you won't have to experience anger at having no one to fix something just because you don't have a spouse!

3. Get affirmation in your life. *Vince joined his friends in a food drive during the holiday season. It was a way to get out and meet people and to get a lot of smiles and encouragement for doing something worthwhile. It also kept his mind off his own pain.*

Accepting comfort from others may not be easy if you have a strong self-image and have not normally admitted that you need love or support. Sometimes, everyone needs comfort and encouragement. You've just suffered an emotional injury and need care, so reach out and allow others to know that you need comfort. Begin to accept the affirmation you need.

Affirmation comes in many forms—compliments, recognition, attention, appreciation, sharing affection, touching, loving, and sex. If your spouse was your sole source, you probably feel starved for affirmation. Right now, the most important person in the world has stopped loving you, so what you receive from other people is probably of little perceived value. If someone hugs you, you are reminded that it is your spouse's arms you want, and you really don't want the hug you are getting.

However, you must build into your life affirmation from sources other than your spouse. It will take a time to relearn the value of these sources.

Don't forget to affirm yourself. Do things that feel good on a sensory level. Eat your favorite foods. Wear a nice cologne. Spray the house with a fresh scent. Rub lotion on your skin and lie in the sun. Soak in a warm bubble bath. Sleep on satin sheets. Wear clothes that make you feel special. Listen to your favorite music (except the sad songs, or "your song"). Go to a concert.

Of course, being nice to yourself and getting affirmation from others may not be as satisfying as what you once received from your spouse. If you regarded them as substitutes, they will be poor ones indeed. They are not substitutes. They are alternatives. Alternative sources of emotional energy and affirmation are necessary for maintaining your emotional equilibrium.

4. Take another look at your spouse. *As soon as he left, Angela's spouse became perfect in her eyes. Suddenly he had no flaws. She could only think of his good qualities and of the good times they would never have again. Angela became very unrealistic.*

You probably developed a fairly accurate understanding of the person you married. However, in the early days after a separation, your memory may focus only on the positive aspects of your spouse. His/her weaknesses don't seem very important now because having the spouse back would be worth living with any faults!

Make a comprehensive list of your spouse's weaknesses (major and minor) as well as his/her strengths. Be honest. Write down everything. Next to each item write how you responded to the strength or weakness. Was your spouse generous? Did you like that, or did you resent the generosity that would pick up the check for lunch with friends, leaving less money for the household? Was your spouse attractive? Were you proud to be seen with that person? Did you also feel jealous when people of the opposite sex noticed just how attractive your spouse was?

Keep your list handy and add to it as you think of things. This exercise will help you retain a more realistic view of your spouse and reduce the amount of idealization.

5. Remove the constant reminders of your spouse. *Sam wandered around the house each evening, feeling the pain of his wife's desertion. As he passed reminders of her, his tears would flow and his heart would feel as if it would burst.*

Reminders of the person you love will rekindle your depression—photographs, birthday gifts, the souvenir from a special trip, furniture you chose together, the figurine you loved and your spouse hated, the outfit that was your spouse's favorite. It is no wonder that thoughts of your spouse are uppermost in your mind.

The most positive thing you can do right now is to remove all of those reminders from your sight. Get a carton and start packing a "memory box."

Important: Do not throw these things away!

Pack away anything that reminds you of your spouse. Include clothes, jewelry, perfume, cologne, gifts, cards, photographs (check your wallet), diaries, love letters, books, newspaper clippings, mementos, stuffed animals, souvenirs, matchbooks. Your home may look stripped when you finish, but that is okay for now. Put the box(s) in an out-of-the-way place where you won't stumble over it (them). Hide large items such as paintings in the back of the guest closet, or in the attic.

Next, change your surroundings and interrupt your memories by rearranging the furniture so you aren't always picturing your beloved in his/her favorite chair. If there is a "favorite chair" that haunts you, move it to the garage or cover it with a bright, new throw. If you are a woman, make your home more feminine. Add bright colors and frills. If you are a man, remove all traces of the feminine touch. Let your home reflect the real you.

Don't sleep in the same bed you used to share with your spouse. You will find it hard to go to sleep, or you will wake up in the middle of the night and reach for him/her. Move into the guest bedroom. Trade beds or rooms with the children. Sleep on the couch. Build a fire in the fireplace and "camp out" with a sleeping bag. Invite a same sex friend to spend the night once in a while. Leave the television or radio on all night to keep you company.

Check your music collection. Set aside the sad songs, recordings of "your song," or love songs. Instead, listen to praise music, worship tapes, upbeat show tunes, or classical music.

Don't spend long afternoons visiting places that were special to you and your spouse. Go to new places: restaurants, concerts, plays, movies, parks, stores, or malls.

Let your friends know that, for now, you don't want to talk about—or hear about—your spouse. You don't need to hear how well or how poorly your spouse is doing. You don't want to talk about your feelings about your spouse at this time.

6. Avoid long periods of being alone. *Duane knew that he would need to avoid being alone for long periods of time while he was awake. So he began to fill his schedule with a lot of activities.*

Fill your schedule so full that you have little time for brooding. Get involved in church activities, classes, volunteer projects, the PTA, community efforts and organizations, singles groups, sports, clubs, or even grassroots politics.

Tackle back-burner projects—things you've always meant to do but have never had time. Experiment with painting, crafts, rug weaving, cabinet building, skiing, fishing, or another project that will consume time and require concentration.

Expand your social life. Give parties. Go to parties and social functions. Cook meals for your friends. Celebrate holidays like you've never done before. Get reacquainted with your family and old friends. Reach out to other people who are lonely and help them overcome their loneliness. Share ideas. Exchange phone numbers and agree to be a prayer partner during this period of loneliness.

Try to do at least two thoughtful, kind deeds each day. Write them in a journal or diary. This record is just for you. You won't be showing it to anyone else. Note ways you made someone's life a little better with a thoughtful word or deed. Do you remember a little gesture of friendship at a time when you needed it? That's how significant your thoughtfulness can be to someone else.

Surround yourself with living things. Fill your living room with plants, or put in a backyard garden. Get a bird, a few goldfish, a cat, or that puppy you've always wanted. Caring for living things will remind you of the preciousness of life.

This kind of schedule takes an incredible amount of energy. You will be exhausted when you finally fall into bed. You will be ready to sleep instead of lying awake dwelling on your personal pain. If you find that you still can't sleep, don't toss and turn. Get up. Read a book. Read your Bible. Pray. Listen to music. Bake cookies. Take a walk. Build a fire and toast marshmallows. Go grocery shopping. Do the laundry. Make use of your awake time. When you feel sleepy, go to bed. If you stay up all night, that's okay. You've been tired before and you'll be tired again. Besides, you will probably sleep well the next night!

To keep busy and avoid being alone is only an emergency, first-aid treatment. It is neither the long-range solution nor the cure. The secret to overcome loneliness and depression is twofold. First, you must develop psychological and inner emotional strength so that external support is not essential to your life. Second, you need to develop a network of friends who will supply the support, love, and attention you need. You can't depend on only one person to provide all of your affirmation needs—especially if that person is no longer in your life. For now, however, these activities will help ease the pain.

Affirmation of Strength

"Because Jesus gives me strength for this experience. I feel strong." Repeat this affirmation several times a day. It is based on the following Scripture passages:

Ps. 29:11: "The Lord gives strength to His people; the Lord blesses His people with peace."

Eph. 3:16–17a: "I pray that out of His glorious riches He may strengthen you with power through His Spirit in your inner being, so that Christ may dwell in your hearts through faith."

Phil. 4:13 "I can do everything through Him who gives me strength."

Reflections

- What new behavior pattern have you noticed in your life since your divorce?
- In what ways have you behaved a little crazily?
- In what ways has your life changed? (Eating habits, sleeping habits, social habits, on-the-job behavior)
- When, if ever, do you think of suicide?
- What do you do to keep yourself alive?
- What areas of your life are you neglecting?
- What relationships could you rekindle or strengthen to help you through this time?
- In what ways do you get your affirmation?
- What things in your house do you need to put away because the memories give you pain?
- What can you add to your weekly schedule to fill up the lonely hours?

Pain-Relieving Activities

As you do them, check off the following "pain relief" activities given in the chapter.

- [ ] 1. Spend extra time praying and reading the Bible.
- [ ] 2. Remove all tempting means of suicide.
- [ ] 3. Make a list of emergency telephone numbers.
- [ ] 4. Avoid being alone when tempted to commit suicide.
- [ ] 5. Rebuild neglected friendships.
- [ ] 6. Make a list of neglected chores and start on them.
- [ ] 7. Build new sources of affirmation into your life.
- [ ] 8. List your spouse's strengths and weaknesses.
- [ ] 9. Box up reminders of your spouse.
- [ ] 10. Rearrange your furniture.
- [ ] 11. Sleep in a different bed.
- [ ] 12. Tell friends not to discuss your spouse with you.
- [ ] 13. Avoid being alone too much.
- [ ] 14. Tackle back-burner projects.
- [ ] 15. Give a party.
- [ ] 16. Do kind deeds for others.
- [ ] 17. Keep a journal or diary.
- [ ] 18. Get a plant or pet to care for.
- [ ] 19. Use the affirmations.

3

"I Find I'm Often Angry"

"Sometimes when I think of my former husband, I get so angry that I am afraid of what I might do!" Gloria laughs at herself sheepishly.

By now you have probably discovered emotions ranging from hope to despair, from jealousy to indifference, from anger to longing. Having run the emotional gauntlet by the end of each day, you feel battered, bruised, and exhausted.

Your thoughts fly from accusing yourself to fantasies of revenge on your spouse. You rehash the marriage a thousand times. You indulge in wishing things were different, in hoping things will change, in considering ways to end your current situation.

The depression stage, the transition from depression to the anger stage and the anger stage, are the most emotionally exhausting of the entire grieving and recovery process. You will be surprised at the anger you feel. Your mood will swing, and sadness will roll over you. You will find yourself embarrassed at your lack of emotional control. You will find it wise to be close to a box of tissue.

You Can Gain Control

Your feelings are triggered primarily by your thoughts. Although you may have removed the physical reminders of your spouse, your mind seems to supply almost continuous reminders. Virtually everything you see or experience is linked to your marriage. Things you never noticed now evoke tears.

And yet it is not what you see that makes you sad; it is what you tell yourself. The airline billboard that you have passed for five years now makes you sad. You see it and say, "I will never go to Hawaii with my spouse." And you cry. A TV commercial shows a spouse going out in the rain to get cold medicine for his wife. You see it and say, "No one loves me, and no one will take care of me when I'm sick." And you cry.

It is time to take charge of your thoughts! They are the single, most powerful influence on your mental and emotional well being! And they belong to you. You can control them.

Of course, at any given time, undesirable and uninvited thoughts can enter our minds. It is our choice to entertain those thoughts, to dwell on them, or to respond to them positively or negatively. We can choose whether to accept them or to reject them. Paul tells us in 2 Cor. 10:5b that with God's help we can bring our thoughts under control and make them obedient to Christ.

Gaining control includes stopping nonproductive thoughts, correcting defective thought patterns, and increasing our positive self-talk.

Stop Nonproductive Thoughts

"I wish I could turn off my thoughts!" Gina admits. "Seems as if there is a recording in my mind, and it is all negative!"

Unless you have discovered a way to stop them, you probably find thoughts of your spouse and your divorce drifting through your mind hundreds of times each day. Even when you are concentrating on a task, you are aware of these thoughts. You experience vague sadness, depression, or anger almost all the time. You think of things you'd like to yell at your spouse. You think of ways to express your continued caring. You think of questions to ask, even though you may not want to hear the answers. Your thoughts about your spouse and the divorce are dominating—controlling—you!

It is time to take control. This is *your* life! The best way to stop undesirable thoughts is to use a process called *thought interruption.*

If you are alone, and suddenly you start thinking things that cause you pain, sadness, or anger, try one of these techniques:

- Yell NO as loudly as you can.
- Clap your hands.
- Stamp your foot.
- Slam a door.
- Stop what you are doing, get up and change chairs, or walk to another location in the room.

If you are not alone, you can

- pinch yourself;
- snap a rubber band you wear around your wrist;
- snap your fingers;
- lightly bite your tongue or lip;
- tug your earlobe;
- rub your nose;
- clench your fists.

Each time you use one of these techniques you tell yourself firmly, *"I will not think about him/her. I will not think about this. These thoughts are not what God wants me to concentrate on."* This affirmation (for that is what it is) is consistent with Phil. 4:8, which tells us not to think on things that are non-productive for us, but instead to concentrate on what is good, pure, just, honest, and of value to us.

At first you may consciously have to interrupt your sad

thoughts several times an hour, but within a few days you will discover you are gaining control over your thought life.

Another way to stop the intruding thoughts is to allow yourself one hour daily to think about the divorce and your spouse. That way, each time you think of your spouse, you can say, "No, I will think about this later."

This is one of the few times in life when a *pity party* (wallowing in self-pity) is recommended. Usually, it is nonproductive to focus on feeling sad, but in this case it may be helpful to express your grief as you mourn the loss of your marriage. Your healing may depend upon it.

So, set aside one hour a day to think about your spouse and your divorce, to cry, to feel the pain and sadness, to wish that things were different. Use a kitchen timer to be sure that you don't take more than an hour, but do force yourself to spend a full hour a day for at least the first week. Don't skip a single day, even if you don't feel like taking the time. If you have difficulty filling the time, then relive your memories—both good and bad. Think of what worked in the marriage and what didn't. Confess your anger and your longing.

With a designated time to dwell on your spouse, you will find it easier to postpone those thoughts that interrupt your day.

To make this technique really effective, schedule the hour at an inconvenient time. Don't wait until your chores are done, the house is clean, supper is over, the kids are in bed, and you have built a fire in the fireplace. This might make the hour pleasurable. It is not appropriate for this hour to be pleasant. Schedule the pity party at a time when you would rather be relaxing, watching a favorite television show, reading, or even sleeping.

It is even recommended that you pick an unusual location and an uncomfortable situation for this special hour each day. Don't sit in a comfortable or favorite chair. Sit in a straight-backed chair, or stand in a corner of a room you don't use much. What you want is to subconsciously associate discomfort with longing thoughts about your spouse. Some people find that they need to go to extremes. I have heard of people who had their hour of grieving while sitting cross-legged on the floor of the attic, soaking their feet in ice water, or sitting in a full bathtub with their clothes on! This is not necessary (although do it if you want), but do isolate yourself from your normal comforts.

Be creative. Find your own mourning space. If you feel angry, beat up on a pillow. Scream. Cry. Verbalize your feelings. Write. Relive your memories. Grieve.

Believe it or not, you will soon find that you just don't want—or need—to spend the full hour grieving. After a week, you will find yourself thinking, "I don't want to do this. I am bored with thinking sad thoughts!" If you keep forcing yourself to have the daily pity party, it won't be long (a week to two weeks) until you won't need it.

A third way to contain your thoughts about the divorce and your spouse is to write *The Last Love Letter*. Use this letter to record all your thoughts, feelings, hopes, and dreams. *This letter will not be mailed!* It simply will be a running letter to your spouse. Keep the letter handy so you can write down ideas as they come to you. Once you have written them down, you don't have to think them any more. If the thoughts surface again, just remind yourself that you have already included them in the letter, and put them out of your mind.

Correct Defective Thought Patterns

Dan developed defective thought patterns after his divorce. He changed. Even casual friends could tell the difference. He became negative, unable to see the positive in anything or any part of his life. He was afraid of relationships, even old friends, believing that since his wife left him, others would reject him too.

In a crisis situation, our thought patterns are often faulty. We are just not "thinking straight." We develop a distorted view of reality based on what has happened. Something terrible has happened, and we begin thinking that life is terrible. Someone stops loving us, and we think that no one will ever love us again. Here are some defective thought patterns that you might be experiencing.

1. Everything is all black or all white. *Robert is caught in this pattern. He tells himself that his spouse is perfect and that he is a failure. Connie has the same defective thoughts, only they are reversed. She believes that her former spouse is a terrible person and she is an angel.*

If you have this problem (thinking that everything is either black or white) you may think that the divorce was *all* your fault, or *all* your spouse's fault. You may believe that you can only be happy if you are married and, as a single-again person, you are doomed to be forever unhappy. You may see the past as totally glorious and the future as completely terrifying.

If God saw us only in terms of perfection and imperfection, we would all be condemned. God's desire is that man and woman live together in a harmonious marriage—and now that bond is broken. (See Rom. 3:23–26.) But He is rich in mercy and grace and, because of Christ's sacrifice on the cross, we can come to God for forgiveness and acceptance, even with all our imperfections (Eph. 1:4–6). With help from the Holy Spirit, we can see others through God's loving perspective and learn to be more gracious and forgiving, not only toward others but toward ourselves as well.

2. Generalizing from one example to all experiences. *Jo has a problem with overgeneralizing. She is convinced that since her husband walked out on her, all men are not to be trusted. She has developed a terrible attitude toward men.*

Although we do learn through the generalizing experience

(fire from a match is hot, fire from a candle is hot, so all fire must be hot), it is not appropriate to generalize everything.

If you are overgeneralizing, you probably tell yourself that since one woman or man has found you unattractive, all other men or women will also find you unattractive. Or since your spouse said that you have faults he/she can't live with, you may believe that everyone will reject you because of your faults. Don't make the mistake of believing that all men or all women are alike.

Remember that God created you in His image and planned long before you were born that you would be conformed to the image of His Son, Jesus Christ (Gen. 1:26, Ps. 139:13–16, Rom. 8:29). You are His workmanship, His design. By God's grace, you are becoming all that He designed you to be. Even the Holy Spirit intercedes for you (Rom. 8:26–27). God accepts you. Others will as well.

3. Focusing on the negative. *Sheila sees only the negative possibilities in her life these days.*

It is terribly destructive if you pick something negative and allow yourself to dwell on it, roll it around on your mind, enlarge upon it, and let it color your entire perception.

If you are doing this, you probably drive to work noticing only those cars around you with a couple inside. You tell yourself that everyone else in the world is a couple except you. You play "yes, but" with anything anyone tries to tell you. "Yes, it is a pretty sunset," you acknowledge, "but I don't have anyone to share it with, and that makes me lonely."

4. Discounting the positive things in your life. *Vance ignores anything good in his life. Life is full of little joys and nice surprises, but people caught in faulty thinking don't even notice them—or if they do, they discount them immediately.*

Do you catch yourself explaining away compliments or nice things people say to you? Do you push away pleasant opportunities, telling yourself that you probably wouldn't enjoy them anyway? God promises to hold you close in good times and bad. Ask Him to open your eyes to the blessings He showers upon you, even when times seem bleak.

5. Forming premature conclusions. *"The only exercise Hilda gets is jumping to conclusions!" a friend quipped teasingly as Hilda made another one of her premature conclusions about a situation.*

You form premature conclusions when you assume that you know what another person is thinking or when you predict the future without having the facts. You are not necessarily right. You don't know the future!

Do you think that your spouse hates the sight of you because he/she refused to go to a party where you would be? Do you think that since your family income is less, you will be forever broke and hopelessly in debt? If you do, you have some work to do on your mental processes.

Solomon tells us in Prov. 18:13 that responding to a situation before having all the information is foolish. Try writing the thoughts that trouble you on paper. Ask a friend to help you take a rational look at the facts. Then ask God's guidance as you plan for the future.

6. Magnifying problems, minimizing your ability to cope. *Luke sees mountains where there are molehills and is absolutely convinced that he can't climb or tunnel through them.*

If you have this problem, you probably exaggerate the problems you face and do not hold a realistic view of your ability to cope. You are not trusting God to stand by you or to give you the wisdom or the strength you need to survive. He has promised to be there for each of us, to uphold us with His hand, and to give us the means to cope with our problems. (See Is. 41:10.) You have all of God's power to call upon. That is more than enough!

7. "Thinking" with our feelings. *Vern allows his feelings and emotions to dictate what he thinks and how he reacts to situations. He is living in emotional turmoil.*

If you share Vern's approach, you feel bored and say your whole life is boring. When you feel angry, you think you are an angry person. Because you feel lonely, you tell yourself that you have to be lonely. This is not always true! Don't confuse feelings with facts.

Feeling isolated and lonely, Elijah cried out to God asking to die because he was the only prophet left in Israel. God corrected him, saying there were 7,000 others who had not yet bowed their knees to the idol Baal (1 Kings 19:10–18). What we feel is not always real, and we cannot let our feelings dictate our thoughts. No matter what we feel, the fact of God's love for us in Jesus remains a constant.

8. Using guilt to punish or push yourself. *Randy uses guilt to try and motivate himself into doing what he thinks he ought to do.*

Do you find yourself saying "I should . . ." or "I shouldn't . . ." to motivate yourself into something, or to keep from doing something you'd like to do? Guilt is a poor motivator. It places control of your actions outside of yourself. Eliminate "should" and "ought" from your vocabulary. Instead, make your actions a conscious choice.

When Joshua challenged the children of Israel to follow God, he didn't say "You and I *should* serve the Lord." Instead, he said, "Choose for yourselves this day whom you will serve . . . as for me and my household, we will serve the Lord" (Joshua 24:15).

9. Calling names and labeling people. *Lynn isn't happy unless she can categorize people and label situations.*

Do you find yourself putting people into categories based on a single behavior or a pattern of actions? Do you think of your spouse as selfish, insensitive, uncaring, a traitor, a quitter, a child, or a deserter? Do you label yourself as unlovable, undesirable, a failure, or unhappy?

You can choose what names you ascribe to people. Try using positive characteristics when categorizing people, including yourself.

10. Taking things and life too personally. *Tom takes everything very seriously and very personally.*

Do you tell yourself that you are at fault for your spouse becoming mentally ill, or for failing in his/her business? Do you think God is punishing you for all your past sins by allowing this divorce to occur?

You are assuming more responsibility than is proper. You are not in charge of the universe, the world, or your spouse. You are only responsible for your own actions. Your spouse is responsible for him/herself (Rom. 14:12; 1 Cor. 3:12–15).

Increase Positive Self-Talk

If you are trapped in these 10 destructive thought patterns, it is time to reprogram your thoughts with positive self-talk. Write down your negative or destructive thoughts. Consider how to turn them into positive, *realistic* thoughts. Even though they may be positive, unrealistic or untrue thoughts will not help you. What you want is a more *realistic* view of the world and what is happening. Here are a few samples:

If You Are Thinking	Tell Yourself
My spouse is perfect	My spouse has some good qualities.
I am a failure.	I have failed at some things and succeeded at others.
This divorce is all my fault.	We both share in the responsibility for this divorce.

No one will ever love me.	I was loved once, and I can be again.
My life as a single again will be unhappy and terrible.	My life as a single will have its ups and downs.
I can't cope with the pain of this divorce.	I can cope with whatever life brings, because I have the power of God in my life.
My life is lonely.	I feel lonely right now, so I will call a friend and see if we can get together.
I should clean my house.	I will clean my house because I like a neat house.

Whenever the faulty thinking begins to intrude, immediately reprogram your thoughts by turning the negative thought into a realistic, positive thought. Repeat the realistic thought several times to etch it into your mind.

Acknowledge the Anger

As you move out of the depression stage of the grieving process, you will find yourself experiencing anger over the divorce and the disruption of your life. Vengeful thoughts are not uncommon at this stage of healing. When first rejected, you suppressed hostile feelings for fear that they could lead to further alienation. Now that you have worked through some of the pain and are further from the initial shock, the hostile feelings will surface. You may feel frustrated at not being loved by your spouse. You may feel jealous that he/she seems to have adapted to the single life with ease. You may feel betrayed because your spouse has a new partner.

When you allow anger to fester inside, you become hateful, bitter, and unpleasant. It will "leak out" onto other people around you. It will color your emotions and thought processes.

It will make your behavior unproductive. You may spend hours fantasizing about ways to get even with your spouse—to the point that you act out some fantasies. You may refuse to co-operate with your spouse in arranging visitation of the children or meetings with lawyers. You may refuse to sign the divorce papers just to irritate your spouse.

Learn to handle your anger.

1. Confess your anger. The angry feelings inside you must come to the surface before you can move on in the healing process. Ask God's help in confessing your anger to yourself, a good friend, and to God Himself.

Start with yourself. It will do no good to refuse to admit the anger you may be feeling. Strong feelings that are unacknowledged will often cause people to become physiclly ill. Are you angry? If so, talk to yourself; write down your feelings. Get them out where you, yourself, can see them.

Suppressing your feelings will not make them go away. It is like trying to hold a beach ball under water. If you aren't careful to maintain total control, the ball will suddenly shoot out of the water, hitting an innocent bystander. You may not like yourself when you feel angry, so you quickly refuse to let anyone know. Here, you need the help of a good and trusted friend, someone you can feel safe with in expressing your feelings. Make time to talk about your anger, to express what you feel. Encourage your friend to respond, not with advice but with paraphrases of what he/she hears you saying.

Allowing yourself to vent your anger freely may lead to dangerous and sinful behaviors. Don't throw his prized golf clubs out in the rain because you are angry that he forgot them in the garage. Don't give all her clothes to Goodwill on the day before she is to pick them up. Don't tell your spouse all the hateful things you are thinking about him/her. Don't fantasize about revenge. Don't put the cat to sleep because you don't want him/her to have it.

Confess your anger to God. Jesus said that the thought is the same as the deed (Matt. 5:28). Allowing yourself to harbor angry thoughts or fantasies of revenge is the same as actually taking the actions. (See 1 John 3:15 where John says that hate is tantamount to murder.) When you find angry feelings toward your spouse, confess them to God. Ask the Holy Spirit to search out your heart to help you see if you are hiding any anger—even from yourself. Choose to give your anger to God. He will handle the justice of the situation (Rom. 12:19–21). With the assurance that Jesus died even for your sins of anger and thoughts of revenge, you can begin to stand before God with a clear conscience.

Divorce recovery can be a difficult process. It may be necessary to involve an additional person to help you deal with the anger. That person may be a professional counselor. You see a medical doctor when you have a physical pain that won't go away, and there is no shame in seeking counseling to help you deal with emotional pain.

2. If possible, resolve your anger. Some things may continue to make you angry, and it is possible that they can be resolved between you and your spouse. It will require both persons, so if your spouse is not willing to work with you, resolution may be impossible. However, you may find that a rational approach—without accusations and with willingness to compromise—may resolve a problem situation.

3. Redirect the energy your anger creates. Anger produces a tremendous amount of energy in us. It is called the "fight/flight syndrome," where the body is physically prepared to run away from danger or to stand and fight the enemy. Either way, there is a release of stored energy. Rather than sitting still, fuming in anger and allowing that energy to go to waste, use it physically to do something useful!

Clean a closet. Wash the car. Weed the garden. Run three miles. Do something—preferably creative and productive.

The next step is harder. You must, in order to progress in your grieving and healing process, forgive your spouse, yourself, and your God for what has happened in your life.

Affirmation of Thought Control

"My thoughts and attitudes are obedient to God's Word. I feel good at gaining victory over my negative thoughts." Repeat this affirmation several times a day. It is based on the following passages from Scripture:

Rom. 12:2: "Do not conform any longer to the pattern of this world, but be transformed by the renewing of your mind. Then you will be able to test and approve what God's will is— His good, pleasing and perfect will."

2 Cor. 10:5: "We demolish arguments and every pretension that sets itself up against the knowledge of God, and we take captive every thought to make it obedient to Christ."

Reflections

- What feelings are you most aware of these days?
- How would you describe your mood most of the time?
- In what ways are you able to control your thoughts about your spouse or the divorce?
- What things have triggered unexpected moments of sadness for you recently?
- How often in a day do you find yourself thinking about your spouse or the divorce?
- Into what destructive thought patterns have you fallen?
- In what ways have you begun using positive, realistic self-talk to help you get through the divorce?
- In what ways are you aware that you are still angry with your spouse?
- What experiences have you had with being angry with yourself about the divorce?
- What have you done to handle your anger appropriately?

Healing Activities

Check off each activity as you do it.

☐ 1. Interrupt your thoughts about your spouse or the divorce.

☐ 2. Have a daily "pity party" for 1–2 weeks.

☐ 3. Write *The Last Love Letter*.

☐ 4. Identify destructive thought patterns.

☐ 5. Rewrite negative thoughts into realistic, positive self-talk.

☐ 6. Acknowledge your anger.

☐ 7. Resolve anger-triggering issues with your spouse.

☐ 8. Use the energy that anger gives you for productive activity.

4

"I Still Have to Deal with My Ex"

"Whenever I pick up the telephone and discover that it's my former wife calling, I feel angry all over again. I want to yell at her, call her names, and demand that she be sorry for what she did to our family," Dennis confesses. *"I just can't deal with her, but I have to because we have a little girl who is only 2 years old, and I want to keep seeing my daughter."*

"I've accepted the fact that my husband and I are getting a divorce," Beverly told her counselor. *"But I really don't know how to let go of him. He has been so much a part of my life for 15 years. I keep turning to say something to him or looking for him to be there to help—and he isn't!"*

When a marriage breaks up, there will be ragged edges of interface between the two persons. The old ways of relating are no longer appropriate.

Barbara explains, "We used to have a pattern of letting little frustrations build up to heated arguments, then making up in bed. Now that we are getting a divorce, we can't do that. Strangely we don't seem to know any other way to handle the problems between us. We never learned how to resolve the little frustrations as they arose!"

Things Are Different Now

You and your former spouse, if you are still communicating, are probably finding similar issues in your relationship.

1. Care issues. It is no longer your responsibility, or right, to take care of your former spouse. You do not do the laundry, the cooking, the cleaning, the car repairs, or the lawn. If you continue your roles from the marriage, you are not making the transition from being married to being single again. It is time to take that step. Each of you must learn to take care of yourself.

(Obviously, if some task or support has been ordered by the court, this must be performed. Examples are spousal support payments, payment of life insurance premiums, and maintenance of mutually owned property.)

If you are the partner who was used to being taken care of, you must accept the fact that you no longer expect your former spouse to fill the role of protector, provider, or parent to you.

"It's hard," Barbara says. "The other day I saw my husband at the grocery store, and when he asked me how things were going, I started to tell him what had broken down at the house, just as if I expected him to rush right over and take care of the problems. In my heart," she adds sheepishly, "I did expect him to rescue me."

In the Bible Paul reminds us that we should take care of ourselves and not lean unnecessarily on others. By doing for ourselves, Paul says we can enjoy the satisfaction of having achieved something (Gal. 6:4–5).

Commit to take charge of your own life and give up the responsibility for your former spouse. List the things you continue to do for your former spouse and decide how to let him/her know that you will no longer perform these tasks. Be kind but be firm. Your spouse cannot continue to depend on you for physical assistance.

Next, list the ways your spouse continues to take care of

you. Decide how you will assume the responsibility. Let your spouse know that you will no longer depend upon him/her for this assistance.

2. Comfort issues. *"Doing the chores alone is not a major problem for me,"* Ted shares. *"What I miss most is not being able to come home and tell my wife about problems at the office. She always helped me gain perspective and comforted me when I wanted to lick my wounds."*

From time to time, you probably miss the comfort you received from your former spouse. When the children misbehave, when the washer breaks, when the bills exceed the income, when the boss mistreats you, when you are lonely, you may instinctively turn to your former spouse, only to find him/her missing.

You realize by now that you must learn to seek comfort elsewhere. Human arms are important when you need comfort, so consider which of your friends are best able to listen to you, empathize with you, and hug you when you need comforting.

Don't forget that you have the best source of comfort available, even better than the comfort your former spouse could have offered. In 2 Cor. 1:3–5 we are told of "the God of all comfort, who comforts us." He promises that you can come boldly to His throne and ask Him to give you a full share of comfort for your heart, your mind, your soul, and your life. Keep coming to Him for more until you are satisfied and no longer in need of comfort.

List the people who can give you comfort when the occasion arises. This way you will not turn automatically to your former spouse in a time of crisis and need.

3. Control issues. Within your marriage you and your former spouse developed a division of power. One may have given more "orders" than the other. One may have learned how to "manipulate" the other into doing what was desired.

One may have conceded during arguments more often than the other. One may have had more of the "final word" with the children.

This power structure is no longer in place. Even though you may still have to relate to your former spouse from time to time (or regularly if there are children and weekly visitation agreements) you do not have to continue living under the same patterns of control and power.

There is a new freedom to make choices for your lifestyle. I remember one of the little choices that was exciting for me after my divorce. It was to wear sandals or shoes with open toes and heels. During my marriage I chose not to wear these shoes, because my husband hated them. Once I was single again, I made a different choice.

You can decide the house rules for your new life. You can decorate the house or apartment to suit your own tastes. You can experiment. You can develop your assertive skills. You can refuse to be manipulated. You don't make these changes to "push your former spouse's buttons" and make him/her angry. You are simply beginning to style your new life.

Take an afternoon and consider every aspect of your life. Make three lists:

- Choices you made in the marriage that you like and will continue to make
- Choices you made in the marriage which you will now change
- Choices you never made before, but will make now

It is time to add a new dimension to your new life. Have fun!

If you are the person who most often got your way in the marriage, you may have difficulty in dealing with your former spouse's new independence, but this is a healthy step for each of you. You are no longer involved in developing a couple identity; instead you are redefining your own self-identities.

4. Communication issues. *Ted is not used to the idea of communicating with his former spouse through a lawyer. "I can pick up the telephone and call her, but either we end up in an argument or she just tells me to talk to her lawyer anyway," he explains.*

Your communication with your former spouse has also changed. You may find that you argue less—or that you argue more. You may find that you are stiffly courteous and polite, almost like strangers, because your new roles are unfamiliar. You may no longer have the same freedom to pick up the telephone and call your former spouse. Your needs may be ignored or, at best, fitted in between the new priorities of your former spouse's life.

Some people find that their communication improves when they are no longer living under the pressure of being married to one another.

It is very important that you and your former spouse strive to communicate the truth in love (Eph. 4:15) as Christians even though you are no longer married to each other. Paul has a lot to say about relationships between members of the body of Christ. He reminds us to put aside malice, bitterness, anger, bad mouthing, and meanness, and to be kind one to another—even to former spouses (Eph. 4:29–32). He says that our communications are to be edifying one to another. This can be a real challenge in many postdivorce situations.

5. Children issues. When children are involved, there is usually continued interaction between the two parents. In some cases it poses no problems. In others, this connection can be a major obstacle to the healing process.

If there are children, and the contact with your former spouse has become a problem, then make a list of the specific problems you are having. Develop a plan to correct each one. Many problems can be resolved or avoided altogether. Here are a few helpful suggestions:

- Don't use drop-off and pick-up times as a time to argue and fight. This is not helpful for the children.
- If you can't deal comfortably with your spouse in regard to the children, then let the children make their own arrangements with the other parent. Be sure the children share that information with you. Of course, this requires that the children be mature enough to handle that responsibility.
- Communicate in writing or on the telephone until you can work through your separation issues.
- Don't change visitation plans unless absolutely necessary.
- Don't use the children to "spy" for you. Don't listen if they "volunteer" information about your spouse and his/her activities.
- Don't belittle, criticize, or berate your former spouse in front of the children.
- Don't try to get the children to "take sides."
- Don't try to buy your children's loyalty or love.
- Don't make the children your new battleground.
- Do be accommodating if plans need to be changed.
- Do be ready or on time for pick-up and drop-off.
- Do let your children know that it is okay and expected that they love both parents.
- Do help your children understand that they are not responsible for your divorce.

For more information on dealing with the single-parenting issues and relating to your former spouse as a single-again parent, you can read one of my following books:

- *I Didn't Plan to Be a Single Parent!* (Concordia, 1981);
- *Single Mothers Raising Sons* (Thomas Nelson, 1988)
- *Dear Lord, I Can't Do It All!* (Concordia, 1991).

Yes, things are different in your relationship with your former spouse, but different doesn't have to be bad. It can be better! You both have an opportunity to change the configuration of your relationship and your communication so that you can relate as adult friends and not as divorced enemies.

This may take time. You may be ready to have a working friendship with your former spouse, but he/she may not be willing or able to relate to you without anger. Or you just may not be ready yourself. That's okay. In fact, limiting your contact to the extent possible just now is a good step.

Don't Kid Yourself!

Karen is fooling herself. She tells herself that she is over her husband, but whenever he is coming to get the children, she does her hair and puts on a special dress. Secretly, she hopes that he will notice her and find her attractive again.

To accelerate your healing, put some distance between yourself and your former spouse. You don't have to do anything drastic such as moving away or changing your telephone number or slamming down the phone if that person calls. Just consciously start pulling away from the former relationship. Later you will want to reconnect and salvage the friendship part of your relationship. But for now, you need your personal space.

Check what you've been telling yourself about your relationship with your former spouse. See if you have been clinging to any of the following faulty beliefs:

- If I am very sweet and considerate, he/she may fall in love with me again.
- If I lose weight, or change my hair style, maybe he/she will see just what he/she lost.
- If I can talk with him/her every day, the pain will be less.
- I'll make him/her jealous.
- I'll make him/her sorry.
- If I never had to talk with him/her again my pain would go away.

- I am so angry I just want to hurt him/her the way he/she hurt me.

Can you see how each belief continues a connection that is not healthy? Break off unhealthy ties and develop a stronger sense of yourself and a clearer definition of your new life.

Look carefully and see—see and feel reality. Let go of fantasy.

What Went Wrong?

Dave looked back on his marriage and on what went wrong. The pressure was over, and the issues were easier to face. He found things he would do differently next time, and things he would want to be different in any new relationship.

As you pull back from your relationship with your former spouse, you will discover that you can look more objectively at the marriage. You can identify areas in your relationship that were unsatisfactory and even destructive. You will see strengths as well as weaknesses. Take note of what you observe, not to place blame but to learn more about yourself and how you behave in relationships. You can become a better person and a more skilled partner if you use what you learn to make changes. Your future friendships and relationships will be stronger and healthier.

There are several issues that break down communication and break up a marriage.

1. Poor communication. *Marge and Alan didn't communicate. Alan didn't know how to express his feelings and didn't seem to have a need to share his thoughts, ideas, dreams, and fears. Marge wanted to analyze and talk about everything—decisions, ideas, dreams, fears, and relationships. Marge felt as if Alan shut her out. Alan felt as if Marge would never shut up. Their relationship lasted five years.*

Problems in communication range from being unable to

express one's innermost self to not keeping confidences . . . from not saying what you mean to not asking for what you want and hoping the other person is a mind reader . . . from using sarcasm, teasing, and name-calling to giving one another the silent treatment. Paul reminds us to not let inappropriate communication proceed out of our mouths (Eph. 4:29). He says we are to communicate with kindness, humbleness, meekness, and patience (Col. 3:12–14).

Whatever the problems were, begin working on your skills. Take a class. Read communications books. Practice new ways of communicating with your friends and coworkers. Don't let the same communication problems plague you.

2. Loss of friendship. *Pete and Judy divorced when they realized that they were no longer friends. They had grown apart during their 10 years of marriage, each developing a different preference so they no longer shared with one another when something happened; instead they called other friends to talk.*

It takes a conscious effort to continue the friendship after a marriage ceremony. The friendship is cultivated with planned time for interacting and sharing with one another. Shared goals strengthen the relationship. The more time a couple spends pursuing different interests, the more likely they will grow apart.

3. Married for the wrong reasons. *Louise and Kevin got married for the wrong reasons. Louise wanted to get out of her parents' house and away from an abusive father, and Kevin wanted to "rescue" her. Both had unrealistic expectations of what marriage would be. When those expectations were not met, their relationship did not survive.*

Many people come to marriage with unreasonable expectations. Which of your expectations proved to be unreasonable? Were you able to discard them, or did you cling to them at the expense of your relationship with your spouse? Take time to list your expectations and analyze them. Maybe a few adjustments are in order, even now.

4. Addictions. Some marriages break up because one or both partners are addicts. Finally, one partner walks away. Addictions may include alcohol, drugs, infidelity, abuse, lying, and even work.

For some, the discovery of the spouse's addiction comes after the marriage. For others, there is prior knowledge, but a conviction that love will break the addiction. This is rarely the case. Without professional help, an addict may never break his/her habit.

5. Broken trust. Many marriages end in divorce because there is a broken trust.

James had an affair, and Ginny, feeling betrayed and unable to ever trust him again, left.

After 18 years of marriage Howard divorced Doris because she had refused to have sex with him for the last 6 years. He felt betrayed. Wasn't sex part of the marriage trust?

6. Mid-life crisis. *Marlene was shocked when Max quit his job of 12 years, grew a beard, let his hair grow long, and walked out of their marriage. Max was having a mid-life crisis and his marriage was one of the casualties.*

Wanda's menopause experience was so severe that she became impossible to live with, and her husband left.

Some marriages are just not strong enough to survive the personal crisis of one or both of the partners.

7. Unhealthy relationships. Perhaps the biggest problem that collapses a marriage is that spouses develop unhealthy relationships. Unhealthy relationships are those in which

- one person dominates and controls the other;
- partners are not allowed personal independence;
- partners manipulate one another;
- communication is guarded and dishonest;
- shortcomings and failures are not forgiven;
- past history is constantly rehashed;

- the relationship is filled with power games;
- arguments are not resolved, just abandoned;
- one person abuses the other;
- partners blame one another;
- partners do not spend time together;
- partners do not share feelings;
- there is no openness;
- partners are not loving one to the other;
- partners ignore the spiritual aspects of their lives.

Our relationship priorities are given to us in Luke 10:27. First we are to love God, then others as much as we love ourselves. We are to be partners, friends, and equals.

Where Do I Go from Here?

As you think back over your marriage relationship and the way you related to and communicated with your spouse, you will probably see areas where you want to grow. Confess these weaknesses to God and ask Him to guide your work on relationship skills.

If you find that you are holding back from accepting your former spouse as a valuable human being who is worthy of friendship and affection, then you are still wrestling with issues of letting go and of forgiveness, which we will discuss in the next two chapters. Pray that God will prepare your heart to begin work in these areas that will facilitate your healing.

If you have depended too heavily on your former spouse for comfort, care, and communication, then begin to develop other sources in your life for these, so that the division between the two of you becomes more clearly defined. Let God become your partner as you rebuild your life.

Affirmation of Having Your Needs Met

"God knows my needs and will meet those needs because He cares for me. I feel independent from my

former spouse." Repeat this affirmation several times a day. It is based on the following passages from Scripture:

Phil. 4:19: "And my God will meet all your needs according to His glorious riches in Christ Jesus."

1 Peter 5:7: "Cast all your anxiety on Him because He cares for you."

Reflections

- In what ways do you still take care of your former spouse?
- In what ways do you still allow your former spouse to take care of you?
- How do you meet your comfort needs now that you are divorced?
- In what ways are control patterns different between you and your former spouse now that you are divorced?
- In what ways do you still control your former spouse, or does he/she still control you?
- If you have children, how are you making the continued connection with your former spouse work for all of you?
- In what ways do you still try to kid yourself when it comes to relating to your former spouse?
- What are some of the basic issues that led to your divorce?
- What relationship skills do you need to learn in order to become a better partner in a friendship or romantic relationship?
- What specific plans do you have to begin improving those skills starting this week?

 # Personal Growth Activities

Check off each of the activities listed in the chapter as you complete each one.

☐ 1. Stop taking care of your former spouse.
☐ 2. Start taking care of yourself.
☐ 3. Find new sources for personal comfort when you need it.
☐ 4. Exercise your new freedom of choice.
☐ 5. Identify problems surrounding visitation of the children and take steps to minimize these.
☐ 6. Identify faulty beliefs and abandon them.
☐ 7. List what went wrong in your relationship and develop a plan to improve your relationship skills.

5

"I Don't Know How to Let Go"

Cindy's former husband has remarried. Cindy knows that she must move on in her own life. Some of the pain has begun to subside, but she still finds herself longing for the good times. Her memories of the problems in her marriage are fading. She finds herself daydreaming about when they fell in love and about the early days of their marriage.

"I know I have to let go of him," she admits candidly, "but I am not sure how to get rid of these memories. When it was good between us, it was very good!"

Letting go of a relationship and the good memories isn't as simple as just deciding that you won't want that person back again. Being in love can be an addiction—we find ourselves wanting contact the way an addict longs for a fix. When the relationship is intact and loving, the addiction can be positive. When the relationship is permanently broken off, the addiction can be destructive.

Not only does it delay your recovery from the pain of a divorce, this addiction gives another person control over *your* life. Control of our lives is something that we Christians give only to the Lord Jesus Christ. Allowing someone else to control our lives gives that person power over us and keeps us from fully committing our lives to Christ. If you are having a problem in this area, you will want to take steps to break the addiction and take charge of the direction of your own life.

Looking even further in your future, a break from another's control will permit you to serve your Lord even more effectively. With God's help through the power of the Holy Spirit, you can be free to serve Him as His ambassador (2 Cor. 5:20). And your life can be an example to others (1 Tim. 4:12).

Don't Indulge in a "Love Fix"

During the first week or so after a relationship breaks up, it is acceptable to contact the other person if you feel a need. You are concerned with survival in those first couple of weeks. You need to do whatever it takes to get you through (as long as it isn't sinful, illegal, or harmful). But you won't get over the divorce as long as you allow yourself to continue to contact your former spouse for a "love fix." Therefore, after a couple of weeks, you will want to avoid contacting him/her just to alleviate your need for him/her.

1. Put some space between you and your former spouse. One of the principles in God's Word is that if something in our lives is a problem, we need to separate ourselves from that problem. In the Sermon on the Mount, Jesus even used the example that if an eye caused us to sin, we would be better off to "pluck it out" than to give in to the sin (Matt. 5:29–30). If the memories of the past and an attachment to a former spouse is a problem, it is best to remove ourselves from that problem until we can overcome it.

In order to break the addiction you feel toward your relationship with your former spouse, it is important to not indulge your need for contact. If you give into your desires for a "love-fix" you have only reinforced your addiction. And the more often you indulge in getting "love-fixes" the stronger the addiction will become. An addict does not break his/her addiction by just having one more little drink or one more little dose of drugs.

Instead, learn to control your urges to contact your former spouse by delaying gratification of your desires. If you walk by a bakery, the delicious smell might give you a strong urge to go off of your diet and have some fresh, hot bread. If you decide to wait an hour before eating the bread, the urge will be either gone or weakened enough that you can resist the temptation.

However, what you do during the hour of waiting will influence whether or not the urge is weakened or strengthened. If you go about your business and keep on walking, running errands, shopping, and eating a salad, you will find the urge to eat the bread is resistible. On the other hand, if you spend the hour standing outside of the bakery, fantasizing about how the bread will taste, and continuing to smell the fresh bread, your resistance will be negligible, and you will probably eat the bread.

The same is true when it comes to contacting your former spouse. If you suddenly have an urge to call him/her, tell yourself you must wait an hour. During that hour, do something distracting. Call another friend. Bake cookies. Go for a brisk run. Mow the lawn. Don't sit with your hand on the telephone and your eye on the clock. Do something that will strengthen your resolve to not be dependent upon your former spouse.

There are situations when continued contact is inevitable—such as when there are children and visitation is frequent. But you can take preventive steps to make unavoidable contact safe for you. Stick to brief discussions of the arrangements for the children. Don't engage in long conversations about your personal lives. Don't try to let him/her know how much you are hurting. Don't try to elicit sympathy or make him/her feel guilty. Ask a friend to be present to defuse the tension when you have to meet your former spouse. By planning to put some space between yourself and your former spouse, you are not necessarily cutting off all contact forever. You are just giving yourself some time to break the addiction you have developed to him/her. Later, when that person no longer has power to disrupt your peace of mind, you may choose to reconnect with him/her and renew the original friendship you once had.

2. Find alternate things to do. *Juanita decided that she had spent enough time crying and wishing her husband would return. She looked at when she was most vulnerable to feeling lonely and needy. She planned ways to keep herself busy with enjoyable activities so she wouldn't be so tempted to pick up the telephone and call her former husband.*

You can do the same.

Get a box or basket and fill it with creative things to do when you need something different to distract you from your strong urge to call your former spouse. You also can rummage in this basket when you are bored or out of sorts. This basket might include lists of local tourist attractions with those you would like to explore circled in red; sewing projects; ready-to-make crafts; books you want to read but haven't; a gift certificate for you to take yourself out to eat; friendship cards ready to be addressed and sent to friends; snapshots that need to be organized in photo albums; or any other projects to keep you occupied.

The basket may also include things that make you feel good—a photo of yourself that you particularly like; an award you are particularly proud of; treasured letters (not from your former spouse); old yearbooks or autograph books; or your favorite sweater.

Planning specific things to do or having reading material or objects that will make you feel good are positive ways to prepare for those depressing times that are inevitable when you are trying to break dependence on someone else to make you happy.

Stop Looking for Him/Her Everywhere You Go

"You won't believe what I did yesterday," Simon told a friend. *"I was driving on the freeway and I saw a green Toyota just like the one my ex-wife, Sue, drives. I started following the car to see where she was going. I went 20 miles out of my way. I was so sure it was Sue. Finally, when I realized what I was doing, I pulled around the car and took a good look at the driver. It wasn't Sue! I felt so foolish! But it seems as if I see her everywhere I go."*

Simon's experience is a common phenomenon among people who have lost a relationship. He saw his former wife everywhere. It might be a familiar car, color of hair, or walk, but whatever it is, the memory of the former partner seems to haunt the rejected person. There is a "startled" reaction. The heart starts to pound. The breathing becomes shallow and quick. There is a burst of adrenaline and a desire to rush forward and verify the sighting. Often an irrational sense of jealousy is experienced, and the person/car is followed.

If you experience this occasionally, it is not a problem. It will soon pass. But if you realize that you "sight" your former spouse several times a day—and that you are following strange people or cars on a frequent basis—or even if you experience the startled response several times a day—you need to take measures to prove that your own mind is victimizing you.

Set aside one whole day to prove that your former spouse can't be everywhere at once. You can't possibly see him/her everywhere you go. Give yourself the assignment to look as many places as you can to prove that your former spouse isn't there. It would be great if you can do it on a day when you know your former spouse is at work or out of town. But it is not necessary to know his/her whereabouts in order to be successful with this exercise. You are not trying to actually run into your former spouse—in fact, quite the opposite. You are proving to yourself that your fear/fantasy of seeing him/her all of the time is unfounded.

Go where you usually find yourself looking for your former spouse: the shopping mall, the grocery store, the restaurant, driving down the freeway or walking in the park. Walk until you can't take another step. Drive until you are out of gas. Look until you get a crick in your neck.

Each time you see a car, a hair style, or a pet that reminds you of your former spouse, check it out. Prove to yourself that it isn't your former spouse.

If you do happen to meet your former spouse, don't stop to chat; you have serious work to do today. You are out to discover just how many other people drive the same kind of car, wear their hair the same, or have the same pets.

Part of the exercise is to be "disappointed" as many times as you can. Each time you discover you haven't accidentally "found" your former spouse, your hopes are dashed, and you are disappointed. The more you experience this little disappointment in one day, the quicker you will stop your automatic response to these "sightings" for now and in the future. Soon you will wait to be excited until you are sure that you are seeing your former spouse. You will have broken the habit.

Plan One Major Mourning Day

"I feel as if I need to have a funeral for my former husband!" Marjorie told her counselor. "Even though he isn't dead, it would be easier if I could go through a ceremony that puts a specific end to the relationship." Marjorie isn't far wrong.

One step in the letting-go process is to have a major mourning day. Set aside one whole day to grieve over your lost relationship. Deliberately plan to make it the saddest day of your life. Some people never completely heal from a deep, personal loss because they never fully mourn the loss. Don't let this happen to you.

Sometimes you just need to acknowledge the pain and fully mourn your loss. When King David's son was dying, David went into mourning. He refused to eat or to get up from the ground where he lay praying to God to spare his child. He fully mourned as he hoped God would be gracious and return the child whom he had been told he would lose. But when the child died, David rose up and accepted what had happened. He went on with his life and later had another son with Bathsheba (2 Sam. 12:14–23).

Perhaps you need a mourning day.

NOTE: If you are afraid that you won't be able to stand the grief, or that you might become seriously suicidal, then you may not be ready for this exercise.

1. Pick a sad date. If possible, choose a date that had a special significance to you and your former spouse. It might be a holiday, a birthday, an anniversary, or the day of the week that you used to reserve as your special time together.

Get out the box in which you packed away all of the mementos from your marriage, because this is the day you will finally go through the box and grieve. You will allow yourself to feel any residual pain still inside. You will cry out any left over tears.

On this day, you will need to be completely alone. So put a Do Not Disturb sign on your front door, unplug your telephone, tell friends not to come over or to call because you will be busy. You may have a trusted friend come over to stay in the house in case of need, but that person must not go through the exercises with you. He/she needs to go into another room and read or do some other quiet activity so you can forget anyone else is present. Having a friend over can inhibit your grief or dilute your experience, and your day of mourning will be wasted.

2. Eat sad foods. The day before your day of mourning, cook several dishes that remind you of your spouse and prepare snack trays with your former spouse's favorite foods.

During your day of mourning, eat these foods and remember the last time you and your former spouse shared them. Take small bites. Recapture the feeling of intimate sharing over a meal, the laughter, and the jokes. Remind yourself that you will never again have those experiences with your former spouse. Allow yourself to experience the sadness of this thought. Cry if you feel like it.

3. Arrange sad smells. Wear the cologne or perfume that was either a gift from or the favorite of your former spouse. Use the air freshener he/she preferred. Burn incense, build a fire, cook onions, or do what needs to be done to generate the smells and odors that remind you of your former spouse.

Breathe in slowly. Let the smells trigger memories of the good times you shared—that camping trip when you tramped through the pines or sitting in front of the fireplace together. Allow the pleasure of those memories to be ruined by the reality that they are over. Experience your loss.

4. Wear sad clothing. You will need to change clothes several times during your day of mourning in order to get rid of all of the ghosts in your closet—his favorite shirt; the bathing suit she bought you; the outfit you wore on your last anniversary; your wedding dress/suit. Try to wear all of the clothes that have sad memories for you.

Stand in front of a full-length mirror. Stroke the material. Remember how you felt when you were happy in this outfit. Look at a photograph of the two of you together when you were wearing this outfit. Smile again at the happy times. Imagine for a moment that they could return again, then let go sadly, as you face the reality that you are alone.

5. Listen to sad sounds. Play the music you used to share, especially "your song." Wind up the music box your former spouse gave you. Turn a fan on the wind chimes you bought together on that trip to Mexico. Lie down, close your eyes, and let the sounds raise hidden sadness from within your soul. Listen to the songs over and over until the sadness is replaced by weariness—even irritation at the repetitiveness of the sound.

6. Touch sad things. Unpack your memory box of sad things. Touch each thing one at a time. Fondle it. Trace your beloved's face in the photograph with your finger. As you touch each thing, itemize everything that reminds you of your lost love. Read the old love letters. Look at your wedding photos. Feel again the thrill of falling in love and the excitement of being loved. Don't go to the next object until you are totally bored by the one you are holding.

You will become bored. The body can only maintain an intense response to a particular stimulus for a limited time. Then the response is automatically adjusted. Diving into cold water is a shock, but the body will soon adjust to the change in temperature. Stepping from the house into the sunlight is a shock, but your eyes will adjust. In a similar manner, your body and mind will adjust to the emotional shock of each item. When you have fully experienced all the thoughts and feelings of sadness associated with that item, it will no longer have power over you.

When you are bored with an item, say so—aloud—in a firm voice. "I am bored with this _____ ." Feel the release. You are alive, it is the past that is dead.

7. Cleanse your heart. After hours of mourning, your heart will probably feel worn out. Read Psalm 51, in which David prays for God to forgive his sin, to create a clean heart in him, and to restore the joy of His salvation.

Meditate on this Psalm and pray a similar prayer. Ask God to search your heart and rid it of the sadness and the mourning. Ask for a clean and a new heart. Ask for joy. Praise and worship God for His faithfulness and constant love. Read the following verses and see what they have to say about giving thanks during hard times: Ps. 51:15–17; 107:22; 116:17; Jer. 33:11; 1 Thess. 5:18; Heb. 13:15, 16.

8. Clean up the mess. By the end of your day of mourning, you will have a giant mess! Clothes are strewn around the room, leftover food is sitting around, objects from the memory box are everywhere, and the trash is overflowing with used tissues.

This is a good sign that you got into the spirit of the day of mourning and that the day was probably profitable in your recovery process.

Now, clean up the mess. Throw away anything you don't want to keep. Hang up the clothes. Clear the dirty dishes and take out the trash. Open the drapes. Plug in the telephone. Take off the Do Not Disturb sign from the door.

9. Celebrate. Write a poem or a prayer to God celebrating all the blessings He has given you. Thank Him for freeing you from the memories that held you hostage. Thank Him for the good times you have known in the past and for the wonderful opportunities the future holds. Promise Him and yourself that you will no longer look back, but that you will look ahead, stretch forward, and strive to accept and attain His goals for your life. (See Phil. 3:13–14.)

Do something special and fun. Go out with friends. Have an impromptu party. Shop for a new outfit. Take yourself out to eat. If possible, do something where you will be with other people. You have survived an emotionally draining experience. You have just taken a giant step in the healing process. You have set yourself free from the power of a whole lot of things that made you sad. What a victory! Celebrate!

Reclaim Your World

After his divorce, Ralph realized that his world had become restricted. In the first weeks after his wife left him, he instinctively avoided places where he could inadvertently run into her. He found a new laundromat to do the laundry. He shopped at a different grocery store even though it was five miles further away. He changed churches. He no longer bought seats in his favorite section of the stadium for the ball games. He stopped going to the symphony, the local movie theater, the community playhouse, and the PTA meetings. He felt bad about missing his son's little league games, but to avoid sitting in the bleachers and seeing his wife nearby, he made excuses for not attending.

There was nothing wrong with Ralph's desire to avoid meeting his former wife while he was trying to cope with the initial pain of rejection and with rebuilding his life. But after a few months, Ralph began to resent that his former wife was free to continue her usual lifestyle while he was a virtual prisoner with all kinds of self-imposed restrictions. He not only avoided the possibility of accidental contact with his former wife, but also any place that brought back memories of their relationship. It was time for Ralph to reclaim his world.

If you are in the same position as Ralph, you need to break free from the restrictions and to reclaim your world.

1. List the places you are avoiding. Take a few minutes to list all of the places you have been avoiding. For example, you may have stopped going to your favorite restaurant because the thought of going there without your spouse has been too painful to consider.

2. Desecrate the memories. Go to each place that holds special memories or fears. Be smart. At first, plan to go when you are least likely to run into your former spouse. "Desecrate" the old painful memories by taking a friend, a date, or a crowd of noisy children. No longer will that table in the restaurant or that box seat be sacred in your memories. It may take more than one visit to exorcise a particularly stubborn ghost if a place was very significant to you and your former spouse. It's important that you enjoy and have fun when you revisit favorite places. Laugh, act silly, relax, and find things to make the new experiences special in their own ways.

Ralph and his former wife went to a special Chinese restaurant on the 15th of each month because they were married on the 15th of the month. It was a romantic, monthly reminder of their wedding. Even if they had been fighting, they always seemed to make up that night. It was a wonderful tradition during the two years of their marriage. That restaurant was last when Ralph began visiting old haunts. He wasn't sure he could stand it. But he took four of his coworkers there one night after work, and they joked and laughed their way through the entire meal. He felt a brief period of awkwardness at first, but soon Ralph realized that he was enjoying himself—and the food. The restaurant was no longer a place to be avoided.

3. Find new ways to enjoy favorite places. If you used to go to the mountains to frolic in the snow, then go in the summer and look for wild flowers. If you went to the park to jog, then take a picnic lunch this time or go out in one of the boats on the lake.

The more times you return to formerly sacred places with new people and do new activities, the more likely you are to remove the threat it holds for you.

4. Rehearse how you will behave if you do accidently run into your former spouse. It is possible that you will run into your former spouse by going to places where you used to go together. Plan for this. Consider what you might say so that you are not left speechless and feeling stupid. A simple greeting and query about how he/she is doing is sufficient. There is no need to explain why you are there, or to make lengthy introductions of the others with you. If you have a plan, and have rehearsed in private how you would behave and respond, there is little to fear from a chance encounter.

Joy and her husband used to frequent used bookstores on weekends. After her divorce, Joy found herself on the verge of tears whenever she passed a used bookstore. One day, she asked two friends to accompany her as she reclaimed her world. She copied the telephone directory pages that listed the used book and thrift stores, and they started out. Through 8 hours of going from one store to another and sorting through hundreds (it felt like thousands) of used books, Joy bought 20 paperbacks. More important, she had rid herself of her irrational response to used bookstores.

When I think of becoming free from fears of going to favorite places, I am reminded of Elijah (1 Kings 17:1–2; 2 Kings 2:11). He was a powerful prophet in Israel, going where he chose and speaking the word of the Lord to the people and the king. Then he fell out of favor with the queen after predicting a drought and later, humiliating the prophets of Baal at Mount Carmel. He ran away and hid in a cave, fearful for his life. At first it was okay for him to hide, rest, and recuperate from his rejection. The angel of the Lord came and ministered to Elijah by feeding him and encouraging him to sleep. Then, the Lord told Elijah to get out of the cave and to go back into his world. He was to anoint two new kings, one over Syria and one over Israel. He also was to anoint a new prophet as his successor.

Back into his familiar world went Elijah with new people, new associates, and a new friend. He was soon back at the palace giving King Ahab the word of the Lord and walking unafraid among the people.

Yes, the Lord gave Elijah the strength to overcome his fears. The Lord gave Elijah new associates and a new friend. The Lord can do the same for you, for He is the same yesterday, today and forever (Heb. 13:8).

Letting go of the past won't happen without effort on your part. You must make a decision to let go, and then take positive steps that will break the ties to the past. Don't remain a prisoner. Become free. Paul tells us in Gal. 5:1 to stand fast in the freedom Christ has given and not to be entangled again with the yoke of bondage. The choice is yours. Will you be free or not?

Affirmation of Personal Growth

"I am growing on a personal and spiritual level. I feel wonderfully free from the past." Repeat this affirmation several times a day. It is based on the following Scripture passages:

1 Thess 5:18: "Give thanks in all circumstances, for this is God's will for you in Christ Jesus."

Phil. 1:6: "[Be] confident of this, that He who began a good work in you will carry it on to completion until the day of Christ Jesus."

Gal. 5:1: "It is for freedom that Christ has set us free. Stand firm, then, and do not let yourselves be burdened again by a yoke of slavery."

Reflections

- What is the most difficult thing, feeling, or memory from your former relationship to let go of?
- In what ways would you say that you may still be "addicted" to your former relationship?
- What do you do to get a "love fix?"
- What do you do to keep from contacting your former spouse for a "love fix?"
- What fun things have you started doing just to please yourself and to fill the empty spaces in your life?
- Do you find yourself "seeing" your former spouse when he/she isn't actually anywhere nearby?
- How might a mourning day help you expedite the letting go process?
- Describe how your world has become restricted since your divorce.
- What places would you most like to "reclaim?"

- In what ways are you still "in bondage" to your past?

Letting Go Activities

- [ ] 1. Put some space between you and your former spouse.
- [ ] 2. Actively resist contacting him/her.
- [ ] 3. Plan alternate fun things to do when you are feeling needy.
- [ ] 4. Set aside a day and prove to yourself that your former spouse isn't everywhere you think you are seeing him/her.
- [ ] 5. Have a major mourning day.
- [ ] 6. Celebrate after the mourning day.
- [ ] 7. List the places you have been avoiding since your divorce.
- [ ] 8. Desecrate your nostalgic and sad memories by building a new history in each of those places.
- [ ] 9. Find new ways to enjoy favorite places.
- [ ] 10. Rehearse how you will behave or respond if you run into your former spouse at a favorite place.
- [ ] 11. Use the affirmations.
- [ ] 12. Respond to the "Reflections" questions.

6

"I'm Not Ready to Forgive"

"Can we just skip this week's session and go on to next week's topic?" Debbie asked, half playfully and half seriously. *"I am less angry than before. I've started to let go of the past, and I'm even finding it possible to laugh occasionally. But I am not ready to forgive my ex-husband. Not yet,"* she continued honestly.

Debbie is not alone in her feeling. Most people who are working through a divorce and struggling to rebuild their lives alone are not anxious to rush toward forgiveness. Suggesting that people need to forgive former spouses for disrupting their lives, for betraying them, for making a unilateral decision to discard the marriage is asking a lot! It is the hardest part of the grieving process. *However, it is the doorway through which one must walk to find total healing.*

Why Is Forgiveness Essential?

Without forgiveness, your healing will be incomplete. Oh, you can go on. You can rebuild your life. You can form new friendships and even remarry. But there will always be a part of your life that is dysfunctional and will continue to poison your relationships—until you ask God to help you forgive everything in your past.

Forgiveness allows you to get past what has happened. You can't deny what happened. It did—and you have been hurt. You can't rewrite history and change the past. It happened. You can't make the pain go away. It exists. You can't ignore the pain because it won't go away; it will get worse. Your only choice—if you want to be healed—is to forgive.

Imagine what your home would be like if you never took out the trash! There would be clutter everywhere. The entire house would stink. You wouldn't get away from the sight and smell. As germs and bacteria multiplied, you could get sick just by living there. No matter how many times you opened the windows, no matter how often you swept, no matter how often you took a bath and put on clean clothes, you and your life would be tainted by the trash you have refused to throw out. At first, only you would notice the effects, but soon anyone coming to your door would be affected by the smell, and eventually the neighbors would know that all was not right in your house.

The same is true of your emotional life. All the anger that you harbor in your heart eventually festers into bitterness that permeates your entire being. At first it isn't hard to hide a little bitterness, much like you would hide a sack of eggshells under the kitchen sink. But left unresolved, the bitterness grows and begins to "stink" up your whole life. You see everything and everyone through your bitterness. If your former spouse left you for another partner, your anger extends to any couple you see together. The bitterness you feel at being alone prevents you from enjoying any pleasant experience. At first only you notice your inability to enjoy life. Soon those who are close to you will become aware of your bitter spirit, and eventually even strangers recognize that all is not right with you.

Forgiveness will get rid of the emotional trash.

Don says he can't forgive his former wife. He thinks of her and his pain on a daily basis. He bores his friends by repeating the story of his betrayal over and over. Don is stuck in his past.

Without forgiveness you will be chained forever to the hurts, the disappointments, and the anger of the past. You can cover them well; you can learn to hide your true responses when you hear the name of your former spouse or the new partner; and you can smile a phony smile. But you will never be free.

When you choose to keep unresolved anger in your life, you make an emotional commitment to that pain. You grant it a permanent residence in your heart. A part of your emotional energy is automatically committed to watching for that pain, for covering it up, for reminding that you have been hurt, and for helping you relive the pain again. The person who hurt you may be blithely going on with his/her life, but you are left behind, emotionally chained to the place where you were hurt.

You cannot complete the grieving process as long as you continue to hold onto the anger and hurt. Forgiveness will free you to release the pain and move on.

1. God wants us to be free from bondage, and this includes being free from the bondage of the past. (See Rom. 6:18; Gal. 5:1.) *Margaret's husband spent the nine years of their marriage belittling her and telling her that she was lucky that he married her because no one else would have ever given her a second glance. He told her that she was stupid, and he made rude remarks about her in front of their friends. After he left, Margaret began to realize the damage he had done to her self-esteem and her life.*

You may have a legitimate reason to be angry and hurt. Your beloved has hurt you—whether it was by ignoring you, physically or emotionally abusing you, or betraying you—while you did everything you could to make him/her happy. And you may have caused anger and hurt in your beloved.

Anyone would tell you that you have been hurt and that you have a right to hurt back. Forgiveness is giving up your right to hurt or to hit back.

Scripture admonishes us to forgive one another. Forgiveness includes repentance. Repentance involves turning away from our bitterness and turning to God. Luke tells us, "Repent, then, and turn to God, so that your sins may be wiped out, that times of refreshing may come from the Lord" (Acts 3:19).

God tells us to forgive because we are not perfect beings. He knows we will let each other down, that we will betray and hurt one another—and therefore, the only way we can function freely is by depending on His help in forgiving one another.

We can forgive because we are told to, but that is incomplete. We are able to practice forgiveness because God forgives us unconditionally through the redeeming sacrifice of Jesus Christ.

In Proverbs we are told to not only forgive, but to do nice things for the ones who hurt us! "If your enemy is hungry, give him food to eat; if he is thirsty, give him water to drink. In doing this, you will heap burning coals on his head, and the Lord will reward you" (Prov. 25:21–22).

Paul reminds us of these verses, and adds, "Do not repay anyone evil for evil. Be careful to do what is right in the eyes of everybody. If it is possible, as far as it depends on you, live at peace with everyone. Do not take revenge, my friends, but leave room for God's wrath, for it is written, 'It is Mine to avenge; I will repay,' says the Lord. On the contrary: 'If your enemy is hungry, feed him; if he is thirsty, give him something to drink: in doing this you will heap burning coals on his head.' Do not be overcome by evil, but overcome evil with good" (Rom. 12:17–21).

Later, in his letter to the Ephesians, Paul again tells us that we are to forgive by copying the model God gave when He forgave us. "Do not let any unwholesome talk come out of your mouths, but only what is helpful for building others up according to their needs, that it may benefit those who listen. And do not grieve the Holy Spirit of God, with whom you were sealed for the day of redemption. Get rid of all bitterness, rage and anger, brawling and slander, along with every form of malice. Be kind and compassionate to one another, forgiving each other, just as in Christ God forgive you" (Eph. 4:29–32).

Jesus put it another way. He said that we are to bless and pray for those who hate us! "But I tell you who hear me: Love your enemies, do good to those who hate you, bless those who curse you, pray for those who mistreat you. If someone strikes you on one cheek, turn to him the other also. If someone takes your cloak, do not stop him from taking your tunic. Give to everyone who asks you, and if anyone takes what belongs to you, do not demand it back. Do to others as you would have them do to you" (Luke 6:27–30).

In Col. 3:13 we are told that we are to "bear with each other and forgive whatever grievances you may have against one another. Forgive as the Lord forgave you."

Matthew 18 calls for us to confront the one who has wronged us. Echoing Christ's love and forgiveness to the one who has hurt us can be the beginning step in healing. Remember that when Christ forgave us, He suffered the ultimate betrayal and made the ultimate sacrifice. As we grow in our faith in Him as our Forgiver, He will help us follow His instructions to forgive others.

2. Forgive because you are forgiven. Forgiveness grows out of response to God's forgiveness in Jesus Christ. You will not be able to move on in your recovery until God's Holy Spirit helps you live in the experience of *being forgiven* yourself.

A clean house is peaceful when it's free of "stinky" emotional trash. For you, the peace is in the faith that God has forgiven you. With that peace, you are better able to extend forgiveness. You have more than your own resources—you have God's help. Through the Holy Spirit, God will help you work through this process of being forgiven and forgiving.

How to Forgive

Forgiveness involves two people. One offers the forgiveness and the other person receives it. To be complete, forgiveness must be offered and accepted. You are only responsible for your part of the process. You can't force the other person to accept your forgiveness or to forgive your shortcomings. You can only do your part of the process.

God is perfect, so God's forgiveness is perfect—without conditions that we have to meet in order to be forgiven. It is perfect because Jesus Christ covered our wrongs through His suffering and death. "For it is by grace you have been saved, through faith—and this is not from yourselves, it is the gift of God—not by works, so that no one can boast" (Eph. 2:8). The hardest part for us is to accept His forgiveness because we think that, somehow, we can make things right all by ourselves. Our faith helps us learn to receive His forgiveness, trusting in His promise, "If we confess our sins, He is faithful and just and will forgive us our sins and purify us from all unrighteousness" (1 John 1:9).

In order to begin the forgiveness process in your own life, you will need to take several steps:

1. Decide that you will forgive your former spouse. *"I didn't want to forgive my former spouse,"* Kim admitted to the other members of his home group from church. *"But one day I realized that whether I felt like forgiving her or not, I had to do so. I asked God to make me willing to forgive.*

The first step for you to take is to repent of your own hurtful deeds and ask God to prepare you to forgive, regardless of how much work it will be and no matter how much you are tempted to stop the process.

2. Commit to forgiving everything he/she has done. *"I could forgive her leaving and the way she treated me during the divorce proceedings, but I found it hard to forgive the betrayal that led to the divorce,"* Kim explained to the group.

Forgiveness covers everything. If you are truly going to forgive, you can't select some things to forgive and continue to be angry about others. Just as God forgives every one of your sins unconditionally in Christ, He calls you to forgive your former spouse completely.

3. Admit to God your reluctance, if any. *Kim knew that he was going to have to discuss his feelings with God. "I just told Him that although I was deciding to forgive my former spouse, I didn't really feel as if I wanted to do so. I was afraid that forgiving her would 'let her off of the hook' as it were."*

God already knows what you are thinking and feeling, so go ahead and confess to Him your fears and reluctance about forgiving your former spouse.

4. Recognize that you also need forgiveness. *"I wasn't the one who was unfaithful in the marriage,"* Kim said. *"So, I didn't feel as if I was the one who needed forgiveness. But then the Holy Spirit brought to my mind the Scripture that says hateful thoughts against someone is the same as murder, and I realized that I had indeed sinned against my former spouse. I needed forgiveness too. That was hard to admit."*

This is a hard step for some people, particularly those who truly believe that they gave everything and did everything they knew how to do to be a good spouse and to make the marriage work. The person who was betrayed and left often does not believe that he/she needs forgiveness. But remember that being angry or hating someone means that you need forgiveness. (See 1 John 3:15.) The responsibility for the breakup of the marriage may be on one person more than the other, but both are hurt and both have hurt one another. Both need forgiveness.

Even the "innocent" party, the one who was left or betrayed, abused or belittled, can be hurtful in retaliation. There may be harsh words, unreasonable demands in the courtroom, manipulation of the children, refusal of visitation rights, withholding of support payments, lies, anger, and bitterness.

Your former spouse may not be ready to receive your forgiveness or to offer you forgiveness, but at this step you need to recognize that we all sin and fall short of God's plan for us (Rom. 3:23). Thankfully, we "are justified freely by his grace through the redemption that came by Christ Jesus" (Rom. 3:24).

5. Acknowledge that your former spouse is a person of value. *Agnes agreed with Kim. "I remember how hard it was to think of my former husband as a person worthy to be liked, let alone loved, after what he has done to our family!"*

No matter what this person has done to you, your children, and your marriage, he/she is a human being valued by God. Begin to look at your former spouse through God's eyes. Just as God hates divorce but loves divorced persons, you can choose to hate what your former spouse did, but still value him/her as a human being.

6. Communicate to your former spouse your desire to forgive him/her and to be forgiven. *This is a delicate step. Fran was angry and hostile toward her former spouse, Wade. So Wade probably will not believe her when she makes overtures about forgiveness. He may suspect a trick.*

Theodore's former spouse doesn't believe that she did anything wrong. She blames his behavior as the cause for her leaving. So she will not be interested in his forgiveness. His attempts may be rejected.

May decided to be forgiving as an act of magnanimous spirituality. So she will come across as feeling spiritually superior and condescending. Her former husband won't be very receptive to her "forgiveness."

Leo acted as if all was well between him and his former spouse, no matter how angry he was inside. His former spouse will be surprised by his admission that he needs to forgive. She may accuse him of being dishonest.

There may be problems in getting together face-to-face. Your former spouse may hang up when you call or refuse to see you. Your former spouse may have made it clear that any communication between you will not be tolerated. Your ex-spouse may have disappeared from your life and you don't know how to get in touch. So, you may be unable to actually communicate with your ex-spouse.

If you can meet in person and have a productive conversation, this is the best alternative. However, a telephone call or a letter will also initiate the process.

7. Be honest but nonaccusing. When you talk with your former spouse, be honest about the hurt you feel about the divorce and your marriage problems. This is not a time to rehash the details. Just say you felt deeply hurt and angry when you were left, betrayed, ignored, abused, or belittled. Admit your anger. Acknowledge that giving and receiving forgiveness will bring healing in your life and improve your ability to move on. If there are children involved, the lack of forgiveness by parents can affect adversely the childrens' lives. State that you have prayed about this issue and that you choose to forgive all the hurt and pain. Ask your former spouse to forgive anything that you may have done in the marriage or divorce that caused him/her pain, and to forgive your anger.

8. Offer restitution, if necessary and possible. *Kurt hired a high-powered attorney when his wife walked out of their marriage. He received an unfair settlement in the divorce because his wife could not afford an attorney. When Kurt realized that he needed to forgive his wife for leaving, he also recognized that he had acted unfairly and needed forgiveness. He offered to set aside the legal settlement and share the resources from their marriage.*

Nancy, whose husband left her for her best friend, retaliated by keeping her ex-husband from seeing the children regularly. She invented "emergencies" and illnesses to punish him for his betrayal. When Nancy forgave her ex-husband, she confessed that she had wronged him by withholding the children and offered to let them stay with him for several weeks during the summer.

If you have done anything for which restitution is needed and possible, offer to make it right. Often, there is no restitution possible for the pain and hurt that partners cause one another in a marriage. Sometimes, the restitution will not be accepted. A wife who has been abused need not accept a proposal of remarriage from her former husband as restitution for his abuse.

Your part of the work of offering forgiveness is now done.

The other half of the process, receiving your forgiveness and offering you forgiveness, is the responsibility of your former spouse. It may not happen right away. It may never happen. That is not your responsibility. We leave the unrepentant to the power of God. He alone can work repentance.

If your spouse does accept your forgiveness and offers forgiveness in return, you must receive that forgiveness. Accepting forgiveness means you agree that you have done wrong and that you will not repeat that behavior.

A Few Cautions

If your former spouse does not accept your forgiveness, then he/she probably does not agree that he/she has done wrong or been hurtful. Therefore, there is no commitment not to repeat the behavior. Offering forgiveness does not mean that you have to place yourself in a position to be hurt again.

If there is an agreement that wrong has been done, and the forgiveness is accepted, then you must also grant your former spouse a degree of trust that he/she will live up to that promise not to hurt you again. Depending on the situation, caution needs to be exercised. Someone who has a problem with abuse or addiction can feel genuine sorrow for hurting loved ones and promise in all sincerity not to abuse or give into the addiction again. Such promises are not usually reliable because long-term, professional help is needed to overcome deep-seated problems.

Forgiveness is a daily choice, motivated by Christ's sacrifice for us, not a one-time event. Just because you have offered forgiveness and your former spouse has accepted it doesn't mean that you won't ever feel the anger or hurt again. It *does* mean that each time you do feel angry or hurt, you will remind yourself that you choose to keep on forgiving until it no longer hurts. Don't "take back" your forgiveness. Jesus told Peter that he needed to forgive and forgive again (Matt. 18:21–22).

Accepting forgiveness is not always easy either! Most of us can look back and see things we did that were not right, and we feel shame and blame ourselves unmercifully. God has promised forgiveness. A partner can offer forgiveness. God will help you participate in that forgiveness and accept it. Forgiveness includes forgiving yourself. Each time the memory of your behavior accuses you, remind yourself that you are forgiven and you have accepted the forgiveness. Don't let the memory control your life any longer.

Forgiveness is not easy. It may be the hardest thing you will ever do. Skip this step in the grieving and healing process and your life will not be peaceful. You will be reduced to going through the motions, to existing. God wants more than that for you (Jer. 29:11) and it is given in Jesus Christ.

Affirmation of Forgiveness

"I have a forgiving attitude toward everyone, including my former spouse. I feel a gentleness toward myself and others." Repeat this affirmation several times a day. It is based on the following passages from Scripture:

"Do not let any unwholesome talk come out of your mouths, but only what is helpful for building others up according to their needs, that it may benefit those who listen. And do not grieve the Holy Spirit of God, with whom you were sealed for the day of redemption. Get rid of all bitterness, rage and anger, brawling and slander, along with every form of malice. Be kind and compassionate to one another, forgiving each other, even as in Christ God forgave you (Eph. 4:29–32).

"And when you stand praying, if you hold anything against anyone, forgive him, so that your Father in heaven may forgive you your sins" (Mark 11:25).

Reflections

- In what ways is it hard for you to forgive your former spouse?
- If you were to forgive your former spouse, what emotional trash would you be rid of?
- In what ways does your pain keep you trapped in the past?
- What pain have you allowed to make a permanent home in your heart?
- How do you respond to the idea that you must forgive in order to be obedient to God? Be honest.
- What did Jesus mean when He said you must forgive others before you seek God's forgiveness for yourself? What difference does this make in your life?
- In what areas are you reluctant to forgive your former spouse?
- For what do you need to be forgiven by your former spouse?
- What response have you had or do you expect when you contact your ex-spouse about getting together to discuss forgiveness?
- In what way will receiving forgiveness be hard for you?

Forgiveness Activities

Check off each of the steps given in the chapter as you complete them.

☐ 1. Decide to forgive.
☐ 2. Commit to forgiving everything he/she has done.
☐ 3. Admit to God your reluctance to forgive, if any.
☐ 4. Recognize that you also need forgiveness.
☐ 5. Acknowledge that your former spouse is a person of value.
☐ 6. Communicate to your former spouse your desire to forgive him/her and to be forgiven.
☐ 7. Be honest, but nonaccusing.
☐ 8. Offer restitution, if necessary and possible.
☐ 9. Accept forgiveness if offered by your former spouse.
☐ 10. Forgive yourself.
☐ 11. Remind yourself that you have forgiven your former spouse each time the memories try to return and hurt you.
☐ 12. Use the affirmation for this chapter, and all previous chapters.

7

"I'm Beginning to Laugh Again"

As the movie credits began to roll, Arlene stopped laughing long enough to dry her eyes. "I can't remember when I've seen anything so funny!" she told her friend. "That was wonderful. I think I'd forgotten how to laugh! It feels good!"

Build Laughter into Your Life

It does. In fact, Solomon commented that a cheerful heart is good medicine (Prov. 17:22). And several thousand years later scientists discovered that laughter releases endorphins (natural pain relievers) into our systems to speed the body's healing. I don't know how it works, but there is nothing that relieves tension and distress as quickly as a good, hearty laugh. So, this week, work at building a significant amount of laughter into your life.

One theme of Jesus' teachings was that life is to be joyful, not miserable. He said He came to give us an abundant life (John 10:10). In John 15:1–11 He told us how His joy would remain in us and our joy would be full. Paul reminds us to rejoice in the Lord always (Phil. 4:4). If your life is joyless, then take positive steps to change it.

1. Videotape funny television shows. *Eileen enjoys*

reruns of old Dick Van Dyke shows. Sean prefers episodes of the Three Stooges. What are your favorite television comedy shows?

If you have a television and videotape recorder, program it to record several funny shows that you are unable to watch at their regular time. Each night before bed, spend an hour watching these shows. Save the ones that are particularly humorous. Keep a supply of these funny tapes for watching again and again.

2. Rent comedy videos or records. *Dorothy enjoys listening to Bill Cosby records and watching almost any stand-up comic. So she belongs to a local video club.*

Rent a different comedy video or album each night. Make a list of the ones that make you laugh out loud so that you can rent them again, especially to share with friends. Buy the tapes that you think would continue to be funny to you.

My favorite movie is *Seems Like Old Times* with Goldie Hawn, Charles Grodin, and Chevy Chase. Whenever I want to laugh and thoroughly enjoy myself, I put that movie on. Although I can almost recite the lines with the actors, I never tire of watching it and laughing.

3. Read humorous books. *Quincy reads joke books. He loves to tell favorite jokes over and over. Usually he laughs the loudest at his own stories.*

Look in the humor section at your local library. Take home several books of jokes, stories for speakers to use as illustrations, and other books classified as humorous. Again, make a note of those that you particularly enjoy so you can read them again. Copy your favorite jokes to share with friends. Read at least 30 minutes each day to lighten your spirit.

4. Play with small children or baby animals. *Vivian visits family members who have small children or baby animals and spends time just enjoying them. Todd goes to the zoo and watches the baby goats in the petting section as they tease the* *other animals. He laughs at the antics of the monkeys and the dolphins.*

You might forget your cares or worries if you do the same and just focus on enjoying the moment.

5. Go to a comedy. *Rex started going to the theater whenever there was a comedy playing. You can do the same.*

Ask friends to recommend movies or plays that are exceptionally funny. Treat yourself to a ticket. Take a friend and laugh together.

6. Play "Remember when . . . " *Bonnie enjoys her children and has wonderful stories about hysterically funny things they did or said. What about your children?*

If you have children, spend one evening remembering funny times from your past. Let each member tell stories as he/she remembers the event. Laugh together in shared intimacy. If you don't have children, get together with a couple of old friends and try the same activity.

If you are reading this book during the first few weeks after your divorce, you probably don't feel you'll ever laugh again. You may not even want to laugh. That's okay. This chapter isn't for those early weeks. It is for several weeks—maybe months—after your walk through the valley of grief and you begin to see a glimmer of hope for the future. Be assured that the time will come when you are ready to laugh again. That will be when you have come to accept your new life.

Recapture Your Joie de Vivre

I watched two-year-old Nicole running around the backyard, humming to herself, laughing with delight as she stumbled, got up, and ran again. "How wonderful to be so carefree," I thought to myself.

Remember when you were young and carefree . . . unafraid of new situations . . . never refusing a dare . . . impulsive and spontaneous? Decide to recapture your lost sense of adventure and find simple joy in living.

Begin by reliving carefree memories. Sit in a comfortable chair, close your eyes, and recall carefree times. Picture yourself as vividly as possible. See yourself in a favorite outfit. Remember the smells, the colors, the other people who were a part of your world at that time. Stop the memory newsreel and relive in minute detail some of these special experiences. Remember who said what, and what you said, and what you thought but didn't say. Experience the feeling of joy and happiness. Do this for several minutes until you have relived several experiences from your happy past. Then open your eyes and carefully answer the following questions.

- What things did you enjoy doing?
- What excited you?
- What friends did you enjoy being with?
- What roles did you enjoy most (mother, father, brother, sister, teacher, artist, actor, musician, boss)?
- How did you gain approval from others?
- What were your daydreams back then?
- What were your goals in those days?
- Who were your heroes?
- How did you think of yourself when you were having fun?

After considering your responses, you are ready to use the information for building good experiences into your new life. Get a piece of paper and *write* your responses to the next questions.

- What enjoyable things can you do again? (List several with tentative dates when you will be able to do them.)
- How can you recreate situations that used to excite you? (Perhaps you used to plan parties and enjoyed getting everything just right. So plan a party for your singles group and recapture the old excitement.)
- Can you call or spend time with old friends who were fun

to be with? (Make a list. Even if you don't know how to get in touch with them, keep them on a list. Perhaps you will think of someone who can give you an address or telephone number.)

- What roles can you recreate and enjoy again? (If your kids are grown and you loved being a parent, volunteer to baby-sit for young married couples in your church. If you used to enjoy teaching, volunteer to teach a Sunday school class, a craft class, or music lessons.)

- What *productive* things did you do that received approval from others? Can you do these things again? (Were you a talented musician, auto mechanic, seamstress, carpenter? Volunteer your talents at church, for a skilled nursing facility, an orphanage, another single adult, or an older couple in the neighborhood.)

- Is there a time when you could turn some of your old day-dreams into real goals? (List the daydreams. See if any might be possible. Plan a trip to Europe, a visit to La Scala, or an interview with a famous person.)

- Which goals can you resurrect and begin working on today? (Start working toward a college degree, a savings account, an addition to the house, or repapering the bedroom.)

- Who are your heroes today? Have they changed from the past? Is there any possibility that you might write a letter to one of your heroes, or arrange to meet him/her? (Try.)

- How do you think of yourself today? Are there thoughts you need to change so that you can once again think of yourself in a positive way? (Make a list and start feeding the good self-talk into your mind.)

Consider what you have written. You have ideas that can add joy back into your life. They are yours for the taking. When you come to the point of acceptance in your recovery, the possibilities are unlimited.

Acceptance Is a Positive Step Forward

"I've accepted the reality of my divorce," Earl assured a friend four weeks after his wife left him. *"I know that we will never be together again. I have to get on with my life, but I can't stop thinking about her. Everywhere I look, I see something that reminds me of my wife. I dream about her every night. I'm so depressed."*

Earl may have accepted the reality of his divorce, but he hasn't reached the "acceptance" step of the grieving process because he is still stuck in the past. Acknowledging the reality is an important, initial step in healing, but truly accepting the new lifestyle comes later on. In acceptance there is a hopeful outlook that moves eagerly toward the new opportunities.

Earl is resigned to his divorce. If he were to remain at this step, he would become resentful of the happiness of others and withdraw into a protective shell to avoid future disappointments.

Alma believes she is in the acceptance stage because she no longer looks to reconciliation with her former husband. Instead, she acts almost driven to find a new—and perfect—mate. She is too eager, too aggressive, and too overwhelming for anyone to respond positively to her. Alma hasn't accepted her new life. She is trying to create an ideal facsimile of her former life as a married person. Alma is desperate.

Jill is apparently taking her divorce in stride. She has a new apartment, attends a new church, has several new friends, and is active several nights a week. She says she doesn't understand people who spend so much time wailing and grieving over someone who doesn't want them. "I certainly don't want to be married to someone who doesn't want to be married to me!" she asserts firmly. "I haven't cried at all about this. I just accepted what happened and kept going." Jill isn't in acceptance, she is in denial.

Acceptance comes long after resignation, desperation, and

denial. Acceptance is a hard-won achievement. When you are in the acceptance stage, you have survived the shock, experienced the denial and bargaining, sunk into and come out of depression, seethed with anger, dreamed of revenge, broken the addiction to the past, killed a few "ghosts," reclaimed your world, confessed your failures, forgiven yourself and your former spouse, and are ready to look forward and redesign a whole new life. Acceptance is a time of hope and anticipation. Acceptance is a smile on your face, a lilt in your voice, laughter bubbling inside, and a sense of excitement when you awake in the morning.

As you can tell, acceptance doesn't just happen at a given time after a significant personal loss like divorce. You do a lot of personal growing and grieving in order to reach genuine acceptance.

Acceptance doesn't mean that you never think of your former spouse, but that you think of him/her infrequently. You don't long for the past, but you may have fond memories of the good times and an occasional nostalgic, but not debilitating, sadness over things that didn't work out. Acceptance *does not* mean that you are not open to a reconciliation should that possibility occur. Acceptance *does* mean that you are done waiting and ready to move on with your life. Complete the following self-assessment:

How Are You Doing?

- How many times a week do you dwell on thoughts of your former spouse? (Less than one is terrific!)
- How many times a day do thoughts of your former spouse flit through your mind? (Less than two is great.)
- How many times a week do you enjoy a good laugh? (More than five is wonderful.)
- How many times a week do you do something to treat yourself? (More than once is super.)

- How many hours a week do you spend on personal development: reading, attending a class, developing a new skill, etc.? (More than two is fantastic.)
- Do you have specific plans for next year's vacation? ("Yes" means that you are moving ahead. Keep it up.)
- Have you written goals for yourself for the next year? ("Yes" indicates that you are taking charge of your life. Don't stop.)
- How many hours a week do you spend having fun with friends? (More than two is excellent.)

If you did not score well with your answers, at least the questions indicate where you may be stuck and what to work on in moving toward the acceptance stage.

The exciting thing is that there is hope for each of us. The Lord has promised that our hope is in Him. If it were not for the Lord, some of us would never make it through the tough experiences. But He walks our journeys with us and promises that we will come through together to the other side. (Read Ps. 23:4–6 and Is. 43:2.)

Remember Hezekiah (2 Kings 20:1–21)? When he was sick he was told by the prophet of God to set his house in order because he was going to die. Hezekiah began mourning and grieving. He prayed to the Lord and the Lord heard his prayer, promising 15 more years to live. Hezekiah accepted the reality and in his remaining years did wonderful things. He didn't stay depressed, he accepted his circumstances, and made his added years a testimony to the power of God.

You can do the same. Start today.

Affirmation of Joy

"The joy of the Lord is in my heart. I feel joyful, and laughter comes easily to me." Repeat this affirmation several times a day. It is based on the following passages from Scripture:

Prov. 17:22 "A cheerful heart is good medicine, but a crushed spirit dries up the bones."

Phil. 4:4 "Rejoice in the Lord always. I will say it again: Rejoice!"

John 15:11 "I have told you this so that my joy may be in you and that your joy may be complete."

Reflections

- In your own words, how would you define the "acceptance" stage of the grieving process?
- How can someone know if he/she is in the acceptance stage?
- How far along do you believe you are in your healing process?
- What signs indicate that you have come to the place of acceptance?
- How do you build laughter into your life?
- What experiences do you enjoy most as a single-again person?
- What fun can you add to your life?
- Which friends do you have the most fun with?
- When do you feel most like praising the Lord?
- In what ways do you see the "joy of the Lord" in your life?

 Joy-Building Activities

Check off each joy-building activity as you complete it.

- ☐ 1. Videotape funny TV shows and watch them each evening.
- ☐ 2. Listen to comedy videos or records in the evening.
- ☐ 3. Read humorous books at least 30 minutes a day.
- ☐ 4. Play with small children or animals at least once a week.
- ☐ 5. Go to a comedy movie or play.

☐ 6. Remember funny experiences and retell the stories with your children or friends.

☐ 7. Relive carefree memories and respond to the questions in the chapter.

☐ 8. Complete the "How are you doing?" self-assessment and write a plan for an improved lifestyle.

8

"I Am Celebrating My New Life"

"I sure don't see much hope in my future," Jeremy con-fided to a close friend. "If my wife stopped loving me and said she couldn't live with me anymore, I don't suppose anyone else would ever be able to love or live with me either!"

Jeremy voices the secret fears of people who have been abandoned by a spouse. People who are in long-term rela-tionships tend to put all their eggs in one basket, as it were, and when the basket is turned upside down, the loss seems both total and permanent.

When Jeremy meets a woman he tells himself, "Don't even think about it. A beautiful woman like that wouldn't be inter-ested in you." So he makes no effort to be an interesting conversation partner or to be charming. He gives the impres-sion that he isn't interested and the woman walks away, rein-forcing Jeremy's self-talk. "See," he thinks, "I told you she wouldn't be interested. Aren't you glad that you didn't put yourself out to try and make friends?"

Can you see the cycle Jeremy is in? Perhaps you are there when it comes to looking at your future. You see opportunities for new friendships, career changes, ministry, and even ro-mance, but you tell yourself that you will never be accepted or appreciated again, let alone loved. Sure enough, because you don't make an effort, no one responds. You tell yourself that it just wasn't meant to be.

God will help you change the cycle! He has never seen you as an unlovable person. In fact, He loved you enough to let His own Son die for you.

Reject Negative Thoughts

Jeremy is afraid of what life might bring (or not bring). He fears that he will never have another love relationship. His fears are expressed in his thoughts as statements of fact. They are played and replayed inside his mind until he genuinely believes them.

Maybe your response to divorce is to think "I will never be loved again" or "I will never succeed again." As you begin to believe these statements, you will act on them. You won't go to a party because you are ugly. You won't go on a date with a new person because you are unlovable. You won't apply for the promotion because you will never succeed at anything you attempt. You won't go back to college because you are dumb and incapable. You won't make friends because you won't ever have a permanent relationship again. You develop negative attitudes toward any opportunity that presents itself.

The solution is to identify the negative statements you are using to torture yourself and hold yourself captive. With God's help, replace them with positive attitudes and affirmations. When you reprogram your mind with positive, realistic affirmations, your behaviors will become more positive.

If you tell yourself that you are shy, you will probably avoid talking with new people, maintaining good eye contact during conversations, going to singles gatherings, or speaking up in a meeting. If, on the other hand, you think that you are a fun person to know, you will not hesitate to enter into conversations, express your opinions, or introduce yourself to strangers.

Your actions are a direct result of your thoughts about yourself.

At first you may have difficulty behaving as an assertive, confident, brave, loving, or friendly person. If so, then ask yourself, "How would I act if I were that way?" Then do so! Soon the new behavior pattern will become more comfortable, and you will see people responding as if you were the person you wish you were. That's because, you will be! You will have changed your behavior by changing your thoughts!

While Jeremy continued with his negative self-talk, people thought he was dull and uninteresting. When he did speak, he spoke so softly and timidly that it was difficult to hear and understand him, let alone agree with him. One day, Jeremy decided to start acting as assertively as his friend, Harvey. Harvey spoke firmly, without hesitation, and people listened to him. Jeremy started telling himself that his ideas were as good as Harvey's. One day at work he tried presenting his ideas with confidence. Although his coworkers were surprised at the change, they paid attention and some of his ideas were adopted. This gave Jeremy confidence, and he expanded his new behaviors. The changes were dramatic and exciting. Today Jeremy has lots of friends and is considered an asset to his work team.

You, too, can change the way people respond to you. Replace your negative attitudes and thoughts with positive affirmations. Negative thoughts usually start as observations or responses to past bad experiences. If you touched a hot stove and suffered a severe burn, your mental response would probably be "If I touch a stove, I will get burned." However, sensible people don't avoid stoves for the rest of their lives! Instead, they become cautious about touching stoves, learning to check if the surface is hot. You change your mental response to "If I touch a *hot* stove, I will get burned." And you learn to discriminate between hot stoves and cold (safe) ones. In much the same way, you want to identify negative responses to bad experiences in relationships and to discriminate between real and imagined outcomes of risking again.

You are loved by God. You will be loved by other people as well. (You were loved once before and you can be loved again.) You can achieve your goals. You can be attractive. Identify your personal negative thoughts and rewrite them into possibilities for your future. Ask God's forgiveness for past faults and begin again. Start risking today.

Paul said in Phil. 3:13–14 that he had learned a valuable lesson. He didn't look back or focus on the past. Instead, he looked toward the future and reached for the possibilities God had ahead for him. You can do the same.

Change the Outside Image

Rose looked in the mirror and shuddered. She had been married for 18 years when her husband divorced her. She had let herself go. She had spent her time looking after her husband, children, and the home and forgotten to look after herself. In the security of her marriage she had become self-neglecting. This was the first time she had looked—really looked—at herself in years. That morning in church the pastor preached on glorifying God with your body (1 Cor. 6:19, 20). He challenged people to consider the message they were giving to the world about the people of God. Rose decided that she didn't like the message she was sending. She was saying that she wasn't important, didn't count, and wasn't worth being loved. She wasn't giving a message of joy and love and hope for the future.

With a little time and effort, Rose could change the package in which she lives. She could become all that she ever was—or all that she *never was!* She decided to take stock and improve her image.

Rose decided that her body needed serious attention. She set realistic goals to lose weight, joined a health spa, changed her eating habits, and started walking three miles a day. She remembered how she took charge of her husband's diet when he developed high blood pressure, and she used that same energy to take charge of her own menus. She remembered how she had successfully coached her daughter's softball team, and she used the same principles to stay with her fitness program. She developed a chart to mark her progress.

Next, Rose checked her wardrobe. Until now, she had focused more on her husband's clothes so that he looked good at the office. It had been okay for her suits to be a little out of style and her dresses to be longer than the current fashion. Now Rose realized that nothing stopped her from concentrating on her own appearance. She took all of her clothes out of the closet, asked a friend to come over, and together they critiqued each outfit. Some were hemmed up. Others were updated and restyled. They decided that new accessories would totally change the look of three outfits that had been hanging in her closet for several years. She matched a blouse with a "new" skirt and vest made from part of an old wool dress. Other things were given to the thrift shop. Then Rose and her friend went shopping for a few things that would complete her look. After a very long day and a lot of work, Rose felt her wardrobe was smart and attractive.

What about you? When was the last time you bought or made yourself a really nice outfit? It need not be expensive! You can find wonderful bargains in thrift shops if you have a good eye for quality and the patience to find the treasures. You might go to a fashion consultant or a color coordinator for advice if you don't feel confident with your own fashion sense. Or just ask help from a friend whose appearance you admire.

Rose also went to a hair stylist for a new look. She was surprised what the lady did with what she had always considered her "problem hair." A little color and a more youthful cut dramatically changed how Rose looked—and how she felt. In the next couple of days she caught herself stopping in front of mirrors to see if that reflection was really hers!

Rose was on her way to a new life, open to the possibilities ahead. She felt better, looked better, and was more confident of her ability to handle her world.

How have you been treating the temple of the Holy Spirit (1 Cor. 6:19–20)? Does it need updating, attention, sprucing up, a little paint, or a new roof? Take time to change your outer image, and you will be surprised at the inner confidence you will discover.

Strengthen the Inner Person

Bill had always kept in good physical shape. It was important to him. It was actually part of his job as a professional football coach. When he felt sluggish physically, he didn't feel alert mentally. So he spent time each week working out and carefully watched what he ate.

But Bill neglected his inner person. He had forgotten that people don't live by food alone, but need to be nourished by the Word of God (Matt. 4:4). He had not been faithful in his personal devotions and on some Sundays he was too tired to go to church. He rarely read a serious book on personal growth or listened to a thought-provoking speaker on any subject, except football. It had been years since he took a class to expand his mental horizons. Bill had been so busy exercising his muscles that he forgot to exercise his brain in any direction except football. He forgot his inner, personal self.

The apostle Paul felt the inner self was so important that in his prayer for the Christians at Ephesus he asked God to strengthen with the power of the Holy Spirit their inner selves (Eph. 3:16–19).

Some people discover during a long-term relationship that they have neglected their personal, spiritual, and intellectual development. The college philosophy major hasn't cracked a good book in years. The idealistic crusader of the '60s hasn't taken time to read the newspaper or listen to the news.

What about you? Dust off some old interests and take a fresh look. You may enjoy a stimulating evening course or involvement in community groups. Perhaps you would like to lead a Bible study in your home—and as the leader you would benefit the most as you prepare the lesson. Decide to read through the Bible this year. (If you read only three chapters a day, you will get all the way through the Bible in one year!) Memorize a verse of Scripture each day. It will give you power and strength to keep on going and to do the right thing (Ps. 119:11).

You will be amazed what happens in your life when you strengthen your inner self.

Take an Assets Inventory

Sally was one of those very organized people. When she decided to take charge of her future, she began with an inventory of her personal assets. "If I am going to design the future I want, I have to know what I already have and what I need to attain," she explained.

Very good, Sally!

Like Sally, you have a wealth of personal assets. Identify them so they can be the basis for your new life. Draw on your strengths and develop new skills and abilities in areas where you are weak.

Start listing every positive thing about yourself, from simply being alive to each of your special skills and abilities. Don't be modest. Write down what would make you interesting to another person. Note your accomplishments. Here are some ideas to get you started. (Have a lot of paper because you might be surprised at how long the list will be.)

1. Physical features. You may not be totally satisfied

with your body, abilities, skill levels, or appearance, but list those things which are good. Perhaps your eyes are an unusual shade of blue or your teeth are pearly white. Maybe you can walk 10 miles a day without tiring or you can win at handball against any of your friends. List everything you can think of that is positive.

If you can only think of negative things, are there ways to turn them into positive assets?

Rhoda had always hated being short. She was only 5'1". One day a man told her that he always felt flattered when they talked because she had to look up to him! The physical act of tilting her head back and looking up came across at a psychological level as an appealing gesture! Up until then, she thought her height was an insurmountable problem. Now she lists it as an asset.

Your self-confidence depends on how you see yourself mentally and physically. Look at yourself as God does—forgiven through Jesus' redeeming sacrifice. Your image is a positive one because of His work in you.

2. Background. *Robin's father had been a missionary to Africa so Robin did not grow up in the United States. He knew little about baseball, football, or famous sports heroes. When he came to attend a U.S. college, he was not up on the latest hairstyles or the current dress fad. It had been a struggle for him to "catch up" with his peer group. He thought of his background as a problem. But actually, it was an asset. Robin could speak a foreign language and had grown up in an interesting and unusual setting. He had hundreds of stories to entertain people. His background was a strength.*

Do you have an intriguing accent, speak a second language, come from another part of the country (world)? Did your ancestors discover gold in California or oil in Texas? Are you directly related to any historical figures, politicians, actors, or actresses? Your education, trips to other places, or funny memories are definitely interesting and have contributed to making you a unique person. Consider your background as a positive asset.

When Paul wrote to the Galatians he reminded them of his background. He had been trained in the teachings of Judaism. He had been a persecutor of the Christians. His background was negative in one sense, but Paul saw it as positive, for when God called him out of that lifestyle, he became zealous for Christ. People glorified God because of who Paul had become in spite of his background. (See Gal. 1:11–24 and Acts 26:1–28.)

3. Achievements. *Jane is a go-getter. She is fun to be around because she is always full of great ideas and not afraid to try them. People tell her she is uncommonly lucky and that they could also succeed if they had the opportunities that she did. Jane just smiles. She knows that luck has nothing to do with her record. She succeeds more than most people because she tries more things than most people. Her friends try two or three new things a year and maybe succeed at one. Jane routinely tries 50 to 60 new things each year and succeeds at 15 or 20. Her success rate is the same as that of her friends (roughly one-third), but her record is more impressive because she tries more.*

Your success record is important to the person that you are inside. When you achieve something, you feel good about yourself and your efforts, and your inner self is strengthened. Fortify your self-concept by listing all your accomplishments, from winning the third grade spelling contest, to getting an *A* in statistics in college, to having your letter to the editor published in the local newspaper. What have you accomplished?

As you write your list, remember that you did not achieve anything on your own. God empowered you, guided you, and gave you the memory, the insight, and the courage to achieve what you have done. For without Him, we can do nothing

(John 15:5). This is great! It means that when you decide to pursue a new goal or to accomplish a task, you can count on Him to guide you. You can pray with Paul his prayer that you will be strengthened and empowered so that in your life God will do more than you ask or think (Eph. 3:16–20).

4. Skills and talents. *Marie has a long list of skills and talents: She can milk a cow, sing, write poetry, play the flute, stitch a quilt, cook Mexican food, sew clothes like a professional, clean the house thoroughly, and entertain children.*

What can you do—Repair cars . . . read at a high speed with high comprehension . . . listen attentively . . . organize a group of people to accomplish a task? Think of everything you have learned to do in your lifetime. You are a talented and highly skilled individual. Don't limit your list. Write everything down.

God has given you unique natural talents and spiritual gifts. These are given to us to use, not to hide or ignore. (Consider Psalm 8 and Eph. 4:7–12.)

5. Interests. *Suzanne has a lot of interests, including some that she has never pursued because she was too busy in her marriage to take time for herself. Now that she is single again she has time and energy to develop her interests.*

What interests you? List hobbies, activities, sports, or jobs you would like to pursue. The first requirement for a new accomplishment is to be interested. Your interest, curiosity, and sense of adventure are assets.

6. Possessions. *Spencer is interesting. He has several unique possessions—a rare coin collection, a piece of ancient pottery from an archaeological dig, photos of his trips around the world, an Indian war club, and a small painting by a famous artist.*

What do you own that might be interesting to other people? Add these things to the list.

7. Characteristics. *Loraine started a new page in her*

assets inventory by listing her characteristics. She felt she could honestly say that she was kind, gentle, caring, dependable, reliable, thrifty, industrious, clean, and patient. As she thought about herself, she added several other characteristics.

Describe yourself in terms of positive characteristics. If you have trouble getting started, read the manifestations of the fruit of the Spirit (Gal. 5:22–23) and write those which apply to you. Then turn to 2 Peter 1:5–8 and add those characteristics which you have attained. Read 1 Cor. 13:1–8 and check out how you measure up to the standard set for love. You might be surprised at how many good characteristics you have developed throughout your life.

8. Friends. Your friends are some of your greatest assets. List those people who love you. List those who are helpful to you. List those who give you honest feedback, even helpful criticism. List those whom you admire and want to emulate. List those persons who give to you and those who let you give to them. Add the names of people who are supportive, fun, adventuresome, and silly. Friends are great assets (Prov. 17:17; 18:24).

Don't forget to add the name of your Lord Jesus Christ, for He is your friend. He does more for you than anyone else ever could or would (John 15:12–17).

When you have developed a complete list of your assets, put it in a place where you can refer to it. It will help to affirm you when you are feeling low or downright depressed. Remember how much you have been given, how much you have accomplished, and how much you have been blessed. Thank God for each of these things on your list, for all good things come from Him (James 1:17).

Set and Achieve Goals

Lee was an achiever. He set personal goals every six months and worked out careful plans to achieve them. His record was very good. If he failed to reach an important goal, he would revise his plan and commit additional time and energy to working on that goal. He rarely abandoned a goal or failed to eventually reach one. Lee knew the secrets to setting and achieving goals in his life.

Are you a goal-setter? Are you a goal-achiever? Can you set them but not reach them? Or do you even fail to put goals out in front of you. Without clear goals, your life may be going in circles, instead of moving ahead in a direction you wish to go.

1. Choose a direction. Goals will provide direction in your life. Perhaps you want to start a ministry for children of divorced parents, or a divorce-recovery ministry, or a choir of single adults to go to nursing homes on Sunday afternoons. Perhaps you want to go back to college to earn a degree in counseling. Maybe you want to learn German. Or you may want to learn to ski, sew, cook gourmet foods, or fly an airplane. You may secretly dream of publishing a book, a screenplay, or a poem. You may daydream about singing in concert or running for public office.

You won't accomplish anything unless you do something about these dreams. I think of the progression like this:

I have fantasies which are nothing more than fun dreams. I'll never accomplish my fantasies, because I don't even try to work toward them. They are usually way out of my current reach and the realm of possibilities.

I have some dreams. These are possibilities which I am not working on at this time. If I ever get serious about these dreams, I will turn them into goals. But for now, they are just nice dreams.

Then I have goals. These are things I am currently working toward. Some are long range (2–5 years), some are medium range (1–2 years) and several are short range (1–12 months).

Good goals have four characteristics:

- They are realistic. *Frieda wants to speak fluent Spanish. She lives in California, and it would be helpful with many of her clients. It is unrealistic for Frieda to set a goal of learning fluent Spanish in two weeks. It is realistic for her to learn Spanish in a year or two if she is willing to work at it.*

  In order to be realistic, a goal must be within your own control. (It is not a realistic goal to inherit a million dollars. That is not within your control.) Also, a goal must be divided into steps that are small enough to be achievable and set over a long enough period of time to be possible.

- They must be measurable. Frieda must find a way to measure her achievement, or she won't know when she has reached her goal. She might put it in terms of numbers of vocabulary words she has learned, the level of books she can read in Spanish, the length of a conversation she can conduct in Spanish, or some other measurable units. Measurable means how many, how often, how long, how much, how high, or other such terms.

- They must be dated. Frieda decided that she will learn 100 words a month starting next month. She wants to be able to conjugate 100 verbs in the past, present, and future tenses in 3 months. She wants to be able to read a third-grade-level book within 4 months, and a sixth-grade-level book within 6 months. Frieda has established realistic dates for her goals.

  Without dates, it is easy to procrastinate. You want to get started so you can achieve. You want to have a date at which to aim. It is important to note that for an ongoing process you set a beginning date. (Frieda will start learning her vocabulary words next month.) For example, if you have decided to exercise 15 minutes a day for the rest of your life, you will want a starting date. If you are going to have personal devotions in the mornings from now on, you will set a starting date.

For a project, you will have an ending date. You will have a new resume typed by the first of the month. You will lose 10 pounds in the next 10 weeks.

- They must be written. Unwritten goals are easy to forget, ignore, or fail to achieve. For best results, write down your goals, develop a written plan for each step toward the goal, and refer to this plan daily.

2. Identify and eliminate the obstacles. *Donna's goal was to lose weight. She had tried several times before, but this time she decided to set a goal and genuinely work toward it. She decided to identify the obstacles between her and her goal. She was surprised to find that there were several things she hadn't considered before.*

- She was a gourmet cook. Because Donna loved gourmet cooking, she used a lot of sauces, fats, and starches. She realized that she would need to become proficient in a new way. Through a class at a local nutrition center, she learned to cook delicious foods that are fat-free and high in fiber. She took pride in how many ways she could prepare green vegetables without adding unnecessary and fattening calories.
- She always had a snack at bedtime. Donna discovered that one obstacle to losing weight was that she couldn't resist a snack at bedtime. (Her usual snack was milk and cookies.)

  Donna began preparing a plate of healthy snacks right after dinner each night. When she was ready for bed, she would take out the attractive plate of fresh vegetables or a sliced apple instead of the milk and cookies. This way she didn't prepare the snacks when she was hungry. It was easier to plan healthy foods right after a meal.
- She bought the wrong foods. Her kids liked several kinds of cookies that Donna did not particularly care for. She could easily resist them. She revised her shopping list and started

removing temptation from the kitchen shelves. It made a tremendous difference.

- She thought of social times as times to eat. When Donna and her friends got together, they ate. Even when they met after dinner, the hostess would provide an array of tempting snacks. Donna suggested that they get together to do active things (exercising, walking, skating, tennis) and that snacks could be low calorie and lowfat. Not only Donna, but her three best friends, lost weight.
- She told herself negative things. In the past Donna started a diet with a lot of energy, but would tell herself that she probably wouldn't succeed. She defeated herself with her own thoughts. This time, Donna told herself she would succeed, and with her planning and determination, she did.

What obstacles are in the way of your goals? Eliminate them and your achievement will happen quicker than ever.

Seek God's Guidance

During this recovery process you have learned to seek God's comfort and forgiveness. Now, as you begin to design your future, ask for His guidance. Think of your spiritual future as well. You are growing in faith as well as in the emotional, social, and personal areas of your life. How can you grow under His guidance?

Prayer is probably the first idea that will come to your mind. God answers prayer. In Phil. 4:6, the apostle Paul tells us not to be anxious but to make our requests of God in prayer. As you pray, ask for guidance as you set your goals and make your plans. Seek His will for your life, asking not just for what you want, but also asking Him to show you what He wants in your life.

Read the Bible for guidance. As you have read through this book, you've been referred to many Scripture passages that have provided comfort. You'll find that God's Word also gives you direction. On one of his missionary journeys, Paul wanted to preach in a certain area, but God blocked the way and, through a man from Macedonia, showed the apostle where he should be directing his attention (Acts 16:7–10). And God's Word gives you hope, for times when your requests aren't answered the way you want them to be answered (see 2 Cor. 12:7–10).

God also provides guidance and direction in the company of other fellow believers. You can find this through attending church, where the preaching of His Word and the sharing of the Lord's Supper will give you spiritual strength.

Put It All Together

You can successfully design a new life if you follow the suggestions in this chapter. Don't let your negative thoughts control your life any longer. You can change your appearance and strengthen your inner self. You have far more assets than you have probably realized. Become aware of them and use them to help you become more than you ever were before. Then take time to set and achieve your goals.

The very last step in a recovery from a deep personal loss such as a divorce is to experience *hope* for the future. It is during this step that designing a future is important. By taking charge we fully understand the potential that God provides for us. We can truly understand and experience what Paul wrote about in Rom. 5:1–5. He said that even during the hard times we can be excited because that is how we grow. We develop patience through experience and trials. We come to the place of hope through the love of God in our hearts. We can become whole again.

Become the person God created you to be. Live the life He would have for you. We, His children, are not to live in bondage, fear, and despair. We are His heirs and joint heirs with Jesus Christ (Rom. 8:14–18). He wants a wonderful life for you. Plan for it. Live it.

The old saying that today is the first day of the rest of your life may be trite, but it is still true. You can have a wonderful future built by you and God. You can become all that you never were. You can live life to its fullest, if you choose to do so. You can accomplish more, enjoy more, share more, and give more as God fills your life with blessings.

Your future is the one that you will design with God's guidance. Be sure to take the opportunity!

Affirmation of Achievement

"I am a unique person who excels through the power of God by setting and achieving godly goals. I feel powerful because I am empowered by the Holy Spirit." Repeat this affirmation several times a day. It is based on the following Scripture passages:

Titus 3:8: "This is a trustworthy saying. And I want you to stress these things, so that those who have trusted in God may be careful to devote themselves to doing what is good. These things are excellent and profitable for everyone."

Phil. 3:13–14: "Brothers, I do not consider myself yet to have taken hold of it. But one thing I do: Forgetting what is behind and straining toward what is ahead, I press on toward the goal to win the prize for which God has called me heavenward in Christ Jesus."

Eph. 3:20–21: "Now to Him who is able to do immeasurably more than all we ask or imagine, according to His power that is at work within us, to Him be glory in the church and in Christ Jesus throughout all generations, for ever and ever! Amen."

Reflections

● What negative thoughts have been controling your life?

- What positive ideas have you been planting in your mind in the last few weeks to help you survive?
- What part of your appearance or physical fitness would you change if you could?
- What are you doing to improve your physical self?
- In terms of level of strength, how strong would you say you are inside?
- What things are you doing, or will you do, to strengthen your inner self?
- List five of your most important assets.
- What goals have you set and failed to reach in the past? What caused you to fail?
- What goals have you set and reached in the past? What helped you most in achieving these goals?
- How have you asked God to guide and direct you as you plan your future?
- What goals will you set this week for changing your life over the next few months?

Future-Building Activities

Check off the following activities suggested in this chapter as you complete each one.

☐ 1. Identify negative thought patterns and habits.
☐ 2. Identify positive thoughts to substitute for the negative ones.
☐ 3. Practice replacing negative thoughts and habits with positive ones.
☐ 4. Assess your outer self. Identify strengths and weaknesses.
☐ 5. Make changes as desired and appropriate.
☐ 6. Identify areas of neglect in your inner self, and give these the attention they need.
☐ 7. Take an assets inventory.
☐ 8. Set short-term, medium-term, and long-term goals, asking God to guide you and develop a realistic plan for achieving these goals.
☐ 9. Use the affirmations.

9

"I Want to Help My Children Cope"

"I wish I knew what to do to help my children cope with the divorce," Dana told her mother one evening after a particularly difficult day. *"I just can't seem to say or do the right things."*

Dana had four boys: Rick, 15; Kyle, 12; Greg, 8; and Alex, 5. Each one responded differently to the divorce.

Rick decided that he no longer needed parental guidance, instruction, or rules. He was ignoring his curfew, hanging around with friends his mother disapproved of, smoking cigarettes, and getting way too close with his girlfriend. Dana was concerned that Rick had become sexually active.

Kyle was angry. He alternately blamed his father for leaving and his mother for not being a good enough wife. He said hurtful things to Dana, whose heart was already raw from pain. Kyle's schoolwork and relationships suffered. His grades slipped from Bs to Cs and Ds. He was so short tempered with friends that some pulled away to give him a lot of room.

Greg withdrew. He seemed to reject any physical expressions of love. When Dana tried to hug him or tuck him in at night, he pushed her away and said he was too old for such things. He appeared to be afraid to be loved, perhaps because *he was afraid to lose someone else he loved. Greg became uncooperative, forgetting to do household chores and homework. He whined and worked sullenly when forced to help around the house. Greg developed annoying habits: kicking chair legs when seated, incessantly cracking his knuckles, and humming most of the time. He knew these things bothered his mother, and he seemed to take a perverse delight in being irritating.*

Alex regressed. He became dependent, refusing to be out of Dana's sight except for school. Staying within touching distance, he asked for frequent hugs. He threw tantrums if she didn't take him along to the store or on errands. He wanted to sleep with her. He started wetting the bed. He couldn't cut up his meat or pour his own milk without spilling it—things he had handled for more than a year before the divorce. Alex cried in his sleep.

Dana was at her wit's end trying to understand what was happening with her children and to help them cope with the divorce.

Like adults, children go through their own grieving processes. They cannot understand what is happening to them, just as you may not feel that you fully understand it all. They may question their faith: "Why is God letting this happen to us? Why doesn't He fix it or stop the divorce?" Children do not understand that you are suffering your own pain as they turn to you to stop theirs. Children usually experience a great deal of anger and fear. To some extent, they usually blame themselves for the divorce and fantasize about their parents getting back together.

You can expect each child to respond differently because children have different personalities and thought processes. But there are some common ways that children of different ages respond to a breakup of their parents' marriage.

Preschool Children

Very young children are bewildered and confused about what is happening. Having one parent move out of the home causes them to wonder about what else might change in their lives. If one parent has left, they reason that the other one might leave, and they develop an overwhelming fear of being abandoned. They may regress to an earlier developmental stage, where the child is more dependent upon the parent. (Examples include bed-wetting, needing help with dressing or eating, inability to do small chores, wanting to be held on the parent's lap, and asking to be carried.) Nightmares and crying while sleeping are not uncommon. Because they don't understand the dynamics of adult relationships and because they still see themselves as the center of their universe, young children usually assume that they are responsible for the divorce. We often hear comments such as "If I had been a better kid, my father/mother wouldn't have left," or "I wish I had kept my room cleaner," or "I'm sorry I used to fight so much with my sister."

The appropriate parental response to preschoolers is to be understanding of what causes the new behaviors, and to practice the following:

- Reassure the children that they are accepted and loved by both parents. Remind them of God's love for them.
- Give frequent hugs and spend extra time at bedtime to cuddle, read, tell them both parents still love them, and even leave a night-light on.
- Pray together before they go to sleep. Encourage them to pray for the other parent too—no matter what your own feelings toward that person are.
- Be aware of their fear of being left, and don't leave them with sitters more than is necessary. Always tell the children when you will be back and don't be late.

- Encourage the children to take care of their own needs to the degree that they are able. Don't rush to respond when asked to cut up a hamburger patty on a preschooler's plate if he/she has handled this in the past.
- Don't excuse the children from the household chores that they did before the divorce. This only reinforces the new dependency and sense of inadequacy your child may be developing.
- When preschoolers lash out at you or say hateful things about the other parent, don't agree with their sentiments, or respond with retaliatory anger. Instead, practice being understanding and say something such as, "You feel very angry with me (or the other parent) don't you? You feel hurt because we are divorced, and it has changed your family and your life, right?"
- Give your children a simple explanation for the divorce. Assure them that you both still love them and that you are not going to leave them. Tell them simply that they are not to blame in any way for the divorce. You may have to repeat these things to your preschoolers, because it conflicts with what they are telling themselves. Each time you say this to your children, you are helping them refuse to believe their own erroneous perceptions.
- Let your children know that they are free to love both parents. Let them have pictures of the other parent in their rooms. Let them call the other parent on the telephone. Let them talk about the other parent and express their longing for the family to be back together again. It is important that the children not have to hide these thoughts and feelings.

Children Ages 6–8

Children 6-8 may have some of the same responses as preschoolers. It is more common for them to experience depression and to become overwhelmed with sadness. They are old enough to realize that the future is going to be different. Whereas preschoolers are aware that the present isn't the same, children who are a little older begin thinking ahead. Mom won't be here to sew Halloween costumes next October; Dad won't be available for our summer fishing trip. We won't have a family Christmas or take a family vacation next year. Children in this age group may develop an intense loyalty for the custodial parent or for the parent who "was left" and an intense anger or hostility toward the noncustodial parent or toward the parent who "left" the marriage. They may not want to visit or talk with the parent they blame. They may develop irritating behaviors to annoy one or both parents in an effort to get back at them and to exercise some power over the persons who have "destroyed" their lives. They may experience conflicting loyalties because there is still a lingering love for both parents even though there may also be anger and blame. Usually these children also assume some blame for the divorce.

The appropriate parental response to children of this age is as follows:

- Reassure the children that they are accepted and still loved by both parents. Tell them over and over that God still loves both parents and the children.
- Be sure to give individual attention to each child, reassuring him/her that you care.
- Don't intrude upon the children when they pull away and go to their rooms. However, if they are spending all their time at home in their rooms, you may need to seek professional assistance for their depression.
- Try to tolerate the irritating habits. In other words, don't give the children power over you by allowing them to trigger angry or hostile responses from you. Instead, whenever they are not doing the annoying behaviors, compliment them on being quiet, calm, helpful, or kind.
- Don't excuse children from their usual chores and home-

work. Encourage them to see that some things in their lives are stable and unchanged. Do your best not to change things unnecessarily. Serve the same types of foods at the same mealtimes. Don't add new house rules unless absolutely necessary.

- Give the children a simple explanation for the divorce. Assure them that you are not going to leave them. Tell them that they are not responsible for the divorce. Repeat these things as appropriate.

- Encourage the children to maintain a good relationship with the other parent. While you don't have to force them to see that parent (unless there is court-ordered visitation), make it clear that you expect them to continue to love and to relate to the other parent. This means encouraging the children to send school photos, copies of grade cards, schoolwork that received good grades, and personal letters to the other parent. Encourage frequent telephone calls and visits. Allow the children to display in their rooms photos of the other parent (and sometimes this will include photos of the other parent's new significant other).

- Encourage the children to get involved in church activities with other children their ages. This may give them contact with other adult role models that will help them during this difficult time. Church activities will also help the children strengthen their personal faith and belief in God.

Children Ages 9–12

While showing some responses of the younger age groups, children who are ages 9–12 may have other problems. Their anger may be more focused. Blaming one or both parents, they may have a list of specific things they believe to be responsible for the divorce. They may spend a lot of time fantasizing that the parents will get back together and may even engineer situations to bring them together so that they will reunite. When they admit that you are not going to reconcile, they may sink into a deep depression that lasts for days after which they may begin new efforts to get you back together. Alternately, they may try to find you dates or ask your dates if they are going to be the new father/mother in the family. They may experience a visible loss of self-esteem as their self-confidence is shaken and they question their own identities. They are no longer sure they can do what they used to do well. They may develop a tremendous loyalty to one parent. They may change in their relationships with their friends and become difficult to get along with.

The appropriate parental response would be to . . .

- Reassure the children that they are accepted and still loved by both parents. Emphasize to them that God still loves each member of the family—adults and children.
- Spend some time with each child individually as well as with all the children together. In this way you can reinforce the sense of family, as well as your special relationship with each of the children. During your special time, read the Scriptures together and pray. Ask God to give each of you strength and insight so that you can build a new life that will be happy and loving. Pray for the other parent. Encourage your child to talk about how he/she feels about God since the divorce. Allow expression of personal doubts and spend time looking into the Word of God to find answers to these doubts.
- Give the children some space to explore and express their feelings—without allowing them to show disrespect for you or the other parent—or to take advantage of the other children in the family. Encourage them to talk about what they are feeling, even if it is anger at you or the other parent. Share some of your own negative feelings and explain that in a difficult situation people must understand and work through their negative feelings. Tell the children how you are handling your own negative feelings.

- Don't excuse the children from their usual chores and schoolwork. Remember to maintain consistent discipline—even when you feel so tired or hurt yourself that it seems like you don't have enough energy.
- Give the children a simple explanation for the divorce without assigning blame. Remind them that the divorce is between the two adults and is not the responsibility or the fault of the children involved. Neither is it the responsibility or place of the children to effect a reconciliation.
- Don't respond in anger if your children develop an exaggerated loyalty to the other parent. Continue to treat them lovingly, as difficult as it may be.

Teenagers

Teenagers may exhibit many of the behaviors seen in younger children. However, they have a unique set of behavioral responses to a divorce in the family. Teenagers often go to extremes in the area of independence. The oldest boy living with the mother may assume the "man of the house" role. The oldest girl living with the father may assume the "woman of the house" role. The oldest child may become a surrogate parent to the younger children, particularly in the absence of either parent.

Often teenagers seem to disregard parental authority after a divorce. This may come from the belief that since the parent is incapable of managing his/her own life to the extent of avoiding a divorce, then the parent is also incapable of managing the teenager's life. Or it may stem from anger toward the parents. Perhaps the teenager simply recognizes that the single parent has less time and energy to enforce house rules and therefore expects to get away with more than was possible before. Whatever the reason, the teenager may begin to exercise a new independence and adopt undesirable habits: skipping school, refusing to go to church, ignoring curfew, refusing to assist around the house, talking back to the parent, drinking or smoking cigarettes or marijuana, choosing friends who are not approved by the parents, dressing in extreme styles, or becoming sexually active. Teenage children may blame themselves for the divorce, particularly if there has been a rocky relationship with the parent who left.

Teenagers may try to get the parents to reconcile or try to match them up with new partners. There may be a withdrawal from the parents and a new secretiveness. There may be serious depression.

Parents can respond to teenagers by . . .

- Telling them, and showing them, that you love them. You might go out of your way to plan a special dinner for your teenager, or to have a party for their friends. You might work together on sewing a special outfit or turning the garage into a recreation room.
- Don't encourage the teenager to adopt an adult role by making him/her surrogate parent to the younger children or turning to them for your own emotional support. While they can be helpful to you, and can assist you in your parental role, don't make them assume adult responsibilities.
- Don't set new and unnecessary house rules, but don't ignore times when your teenagers disregard existing rules. You still need to exercise consistent discipline, even though there isn't another adult in the house to back you up.
- Give the teenager an explanation for the divorce, and reassure him/her that the responsibility for the divorce belongs to the two parents and not the children. Remind them that your dating life is your responsibility and not theirs. Acknowledge that you may someday begin dating and may even fall in love again, but when, and if, that happens, you will discuss it with them.
- Give your teenager some space to be alone and don't intrude unnecessarily into his/her room.

- Encourage your teenager to seek comfort in the Word of God and to strengthen his/her faith. Be sure to demonstrate your own faith by your life. Don't stop attending your church, reading the Word of God, or praying with the family.

Adult Children

The response of adult children to their parents' divorce is often surprising. While a few are accepting and even ask, "Why did you wait so long?" most are upset. You are changing their picture of their parents, and they don't like it. They may want you to have stayed together even if you aren't happy or have no choice in the matter. They may assign blame to one or both parents. They may take sides and even turn completely away from one or both parents. They may develop an exaggerated fear of being divorced themselves, to the extent of postponing their own marriages. Their faith may be challenged as they wonder how Christian parents can teach one way of life and behave in another.

The best way to respond to adult children is to . . .

- Reassure them that you still love them.
- Remind them that God still loves each of you and that there is forgiveness for our failures as we confess them to God.
- Give them an explanation for the divorce and don't encourage them to take sides but to accept and continue to love both parents.
- Allow them to express their negative thoughts and feelings as long as they don't show disrespect for you or the other parent. Do encourage them to consider both sides and different points of view about the situation.
- Don't try to force them to accept you or to spend time with you, but be sure to leave the door open for them to come back to you when they have worked through their anger and hurt.

Adaptive Children of Any Age

Some displays of depression, anger, and hostility are normal and can be expected in children of any age. Occasionally, children will develop behaviors that are exactly the opposite. They will become, in transactional analysis terms, "adaptive children." They will become *too good*. Their rooms are immaculate. Their dresser drawers are organized and neat. They excel in school. They are helpful, kind, and sweet. They keep their clothes clean. They don't make messes. They take on extra chores and even wait on the parent by bringing glasses of iced tea or cups of coffee. In public, these children are a joy, never interrupting, always polite, and smiling sweetly.

If your child has suddenly become an angel instead of a normal little child, then you may need to take a closer look. Children who are *too good* are usually denying or internalizing their anger and fears. They are trying very hard not to anger anyone so there won't be additional rejection. They are usually experiencing an irrational fear of rejection and assuming all of the blame for the divorce. They don't want to cause anything else bad to happen, so they are being as good as they can. Living with such tremendous fear or guilt without resolution can cause your child to grow up with an unrealistic view of him/herself and with unrealistic expectations about life. Adults who grew up as adaptive children have low self-esteem, have an exaggerated need for attention and approval, are people pleasers, are unable to deal with fear, are envious of others who can speak their minds, and often have secret desires to do things that they consider to be prohibited.

This is not to say that if you have a good child, that you have to be worried and rush him/her off to a Christian psychologist or psychiatrist. But be aware that a child who is too good may be having serious problems and may need professional help.

Understand the Losses

When a divorce occurs in a family with children, the children experience significant losses. It is important that we as parents understand what our children are going through in order to help them.

In a divorce situation, children may experience these losses:

- A family with two parents in the home.
- Their former lifestyle. There may be less income in the family, so there are fewer luxuries, vacations, clothes, and outings.
- A move to another home. Reduced income may force a move to a less expensive home or apartment. Potential losses are many—a familiar home, contact with neighborhood friends, their own room, a familiar school, favorite teachers and coaches.
- Fantasies about marriage and people "living happily ever after."
- Comfort and security.
- Personal self-esteem.

These losses are as significant to the children as the losses adults experience. Sensitivity to their losses will enable you to help them cope. Children cannot be expected to just pick up the pieces and walk on as if nothing has happened. They are justifiably angry and hurt. They feel powerless—as if they can control nothing in their lives. This is often why they behave disruptively. They are trying to exercise some control over at least a portion of their lives.

Help Them Grieve

As you actively work through your grieving process, remember that the children also need to go through their own grieving cycle.

There are some good materials available that will help you help your children:

- *Children of Divorce* by Jim and Barbara Dycus (David C. Cook Publishing Co., 1987);
- *Children and Divorce* by Archibald D. Hart (Word, 1985);
- *The Adult Child of Divorce* by Bob Burns and Michael J. Brissett, Jr. (Thomas Nelson Publishers, 1991);
- *Developing a Single-Parent Family Ministry: The Complete Resource For Your Church* by Barbara Schiller (NavPress, 1992).

Don't be afraid to seek professional help from a qualified, Christian counselor. You may not be the best person to draw out your children and to facilitate their healing. A counselor is trained to help. If you cannot afford a counselor, talk to your school principal, pastor, or social services worker. They may be able to direct you to a counselor whose charges will be based on your ability to pay, or even given on a pro bono basis.

Don't expect your children to just "get over" the divorce. In time, their initial response to the divorce will be less emotional, but they need to do more than just stuff their feelings down inside and get on with living. They need to fully mourn their losses and to work through the same grief cycle as you do. So, help them express their negative feelings and thoughts (even when you don't like what you are hearing). Help them turn their anger and blame over to God and confess thoughts of revenge and punishment. Assist them to practice forgiveness as you model a forgiving spirit. Encourage them to maintain a good relationship with the other parent (and the new step-parent if there is one). Encourage them to let go of the past and to build a new future together with you.

Don't be afraid that your children are damaged for life because of the divorce or because of flawed behavior exhibited by you and your former spouse. Dana was afraid that her boys would become alcoholics like their dad or develop a record of unfaithfulness like him. The sins of the parents are not necessarily lived out in the lives of the children. Children may tend to copy behaviors they see in their parents, but they are not doomed to live out the same lifestyles. By providing good training, we can ensure that our children are brought up to know what is right and good. We can claim the promise of Prov. 22:6: "Train up a child in the way he should go, and when he is old he will not turn from it."

Count on God to be the "missing" parent in your children's lives. He has promised to

- deliver the "fatherless"—a term that actually means the abandoned, so it applies to the "motherless" also (Job 29:12);
- help the "fatherless" (Ps. 10:14);
- be a "father" to the "fatherless" (Ps. 68:5);
- defend the "fatherless" (Ps. 82:3);
- relieve the "fatherless" (Ps. 146:9).

Turn to your church to provide assistance. If there is no program for single parents, then get together with other single parents and start a group. Let men provide male role models for children and women provide female role models. Share outgrown clothing and toys with one another. Baby-sit for one another. Get together and talk about your feelings, and do Bible studies on discipline and grief and joy. Work on projects together. But most of all, provide families to help your children grieve. God's Word also gives instructions on how to relate to the "fatherless" or abandoned children:

- Do not take advantage of them (Ex. 22:22);
- Share food and supplies with them (Deut. 24:19–24);
- Give money to support them (Deut. 26:12);

- Look after them (James 1:27).

Do take time to teach your children about spiritual things and to help them grow in their faith. Be sure your children feel secure in God's love. Explain again that the divorce is not your children's fault, nor is God punishing them for anything they did. God sent Jesus to die on the cross to take all the punishment for mistakes that moms and dads and kids make. Pray often with your children. Thank God for His love. And assure your children that both you and your former spouse will always love them.

As you seek to train them in the ways you wish them to adopt, be sure that you are kind and do not provoke them. Seek to bring them up in the "nurture and admonition of the Lord" (Eph. 6:4 KJV). While you will not be able to make your children's choices for them, you will raise wise children for they will delight your heart (Prov. 10:1).

Enjoy your children. Find moments of joy and laugh together. Spend time loving, cuddling, playing together. Nothing can substitute for memories of good times with your parents, especially during a difficult experience such as a divorce.

Affirmation of Wisdom

"I am a wise parent who is gentle and understanding with my children. I feel good about helping them cope with difficult times." Repeat this affirmation several times a day. It is based on the following Scripture passages:

James 1:5 "If any of you lacks wisdom, he should ask God, who gives generously to all without finding fault, and it will be given to him."

Prov. 22:6 "Train up a child in the way he should go, and when he is old he will not turn from it."

Prov. 29:15 "The rod of correction imparts wisdom, but a child left to himself disgraces his mother."

Matt. 19:14 "Jesus said, 'Let the little children come to me, and do not hinder them, for the kingdom of heaven belongs to such as these.' "

Reflections

- In what ways can you identify with Dana and the responses of her children?
- Describe the behavioral responses of your children to the divorce.
- What things are you doing to help each child get through this time?
- In what ways do you respond to your child's anger? What is your instinctive response as compared to your actual response?
- How do you encourage your children to maintain a relationship with the other parent?
- In what ways are you actively encouraging your child to maintain a strong personal faith in God?
- What have you done to mitigate the losses your child(ren) has/have experienced?
- How could a professional Christian counselor assist your family?
- In what ways has the church assisted you and your children?
- How can you reach out to other children of divorced parents and assist them?

 # Activities to Help the Children

Check off the following activities for helping your children cope as you complete each one.

1. Express your continuing love.
2. Reassure your children of the continuing love of the other parent.
3. Reassure your children that God still loves each of the parents and the children.
4. Express your love physically and with your actions.
5. When you leave your children, return when you say you will.
6. Don't reinforce regressive behaviors in the children.
7. Expect children to continue doing their household chores.
8. Allow children to express negative thoughts and feelings as long as there is no disrespect to the parents.
9. Give children a simple explanation of the divorce.
10. Reassure the children that they are not responsible for the divorce, for a reconciliation, or for matching you up with a new partner.
11. Encourage the children to maintain a positive relationship with the other parent.
12. Spend time with each child individually, as well as time with all children together.
13. Allow children some private, quiet time to think and to be alone.
14. Encourage children to develop and maintain a strong personal faith.
15. Provide clear house rules and consistent, fair discipline.
16. Seek professional assistance when necessary.
17. Seek assistance from the church.
18. Get together with other single-parent families for support, sharing, and fun.
19. Find ways to enjoy the children and to make their lives fun.

10

"I May Someday Love Again"

When I was first divorced, I thought that the word *marriage* could be removed from the dictionary because I was never going to use it again. Marriage meant hurt and pain and rejection, and I didn't want any more in my life.

Fortunately for me, I met a guy at work who felt exactly the same way. In fact, our first conversation was comical. He invited me for a cup of coffee at break time, but let me know that he wasn't interested in a serious relationship. At any other time in my life I might have been offended by the comment, but now I was reassured! I responded by saying that I did not want any relationship that faintly resembled a romance.

So we had coffee, and we hit it off very well. It was great to talk with a man and not be concerned about the male-female undercurrents. We became good friends.

Soon we took our coffee breaks together every day. Breaks were so short that often we had to interrupt a conversation to return to work. So, of course, we solved that by having lunch together. But, even that was limiting, and within a couple of months we were spending long blocks of time together on the weekends. Within several weeks, we were getting together a couple of times a week for dinner. Two and a half years later we realized that we were talking about marriage as a distinct possibility for us. I was surprised. I also realized that I had changed my mind about remarrying. I was seriously considering it. Even though we decided not to marry one another, I had healed to the point of being ready to fall in love again.

You may feel, as I did, that falling in love again is the last thing you ever want to do. Or you may already have worked through your grieving process and are ready to start dating.

Don't Rush into a New Relationship

Apart from the initial loneliness of being newly uncoupled is our underlying desire to love and be loved by a person of the opposite sex. When that is missing, even the most supportive friendships will sometimes feel inadequate. But don't let your need to love and be loved propel you into a new relationship too quickly. Go slowly.

Going slowly is a problem for Alice. Whenever she starts dating a guy she assumes that this relationship is going to last. Because the pain of being alone is suspended temporarily, she believes that this is genuine and lasting love. She begins making permanent plans. She sends out holiday cards and signs both of their names as if they were already a couple. Alice rushes the relationship by seeking instant intimacy. She shares her life story, her secret dreams, and her fears. Like a person who closes her eyes and dives into an unfamiliar river, she often finds the waters filled with painful surprises. She scares most men off and ends up being rejected every couple of months.

Starting a new relationship can be an exciting time. Enjoy the process but don't be in a hurry. Take the steps that ensure you do your part to make the new relationship better than your past relationship(s).

Critique Your Past Relationship

Nathan had been married to a woman who made life miserable for anyone who didn't go along with her ideas. He

*learned to cope by being acquiescent unless an issue was ter-
ribly important to him. Because of this he developed a passive-
aggressive approach to relationships. He never learned how
to confront constructively in a loving relationship. He had been
unable to express his opinion about anything in the home, and
as a result, had no confidence in any of his ideas and pref-
erences for decorating style.*

Now that Nathan is single again, he has an opportunity to
develop skills to function better in a partnership relationship.
He has to recognize that without new skills, he will behave
much the same in a new relationship as he did in his past
relationship(s). Unless he makes a conscious decision, Nathan,
like most people, will tend to be attracted to someone much
like his former spouse. Even if he doesn't select someone with
the same behaviors, the new woman will develop behaviors
similar to his former spouse unless Nathan's own behavior
changes.

In other words, if Nathan never speaks up in his new relationship, the new person will, by default, take charge of their
lives. When something is important enough for Nathan to take
a stand, he will anticipate a disagreement and adopt a defensive
argumentative posture. That will probably precipitate an unnecessary argument.

You are encouraged to assess your resources and potential
before starting a new relationship. In Luke 14:27–30, Jesus
describes how planning is important. In this section, He is telling
the crowds to consider what may happen if they associate with
Him. You can use His advice to look at yourself and your
future relationships.

Get a pencil and paper and write out your responses to
the following questions. Make notes that will help you consider
the past as a training ground for the future. When you have
finished, share your responses with a trusted friend. You may
be too hard on yourself, or you may not have enough insight
to pinpoint problems to avoid.

Once you have completed the assessment, develop a plan for tackling each area you want to change to improve your relationship skills. What things can you improve from your former marriage to give a new marriage a better chance at succeeding?

1. Did you lack a strong supportive group of friends? Did you consider your spouse your best—and only—friend? This may have placed a heavy burden on your spouse, for no one can be all things to another person. Even married people need their own friends, separate from those who are friends of the couple. This lack of other friends may have made you jealous of any time your spouse spent apart from you, even when concentrating on a personal project.

Even Jesus had many friends. He ate with some, visited with others, walked with many, and took some to special places, such as when Peter, James, and John were with Him on the Mount of Transfiguration (Matt. 17:1–13). He didn't expect just one person to do everything with Him or to be His only friend.

2. Did you have mutual goals? A couple can build depth and strength into their relationship when they establish mutual goals: building a deck, saving for a vacation, getting out of debt, putting each other through college, or learning how to cook gourmet meals. Other couples may have different goals. Without mutual goals a couple may find their lives growing in directions that conflict with one another and eventually destroy the marriage. If her goal is to have the most fancy home and his is to save for a boat, there will probably be arguments, unless there is enough money for both. However, a loving couple will sit down and discuss goals that conflict and make compromises. They may decide to decorate the house first and then buy the boat. Or they may decide to save so much a month, half for the house and half for the boat.

When Jana was first married, she wanted to buy little sur-

prises for her husband, but all he wanted was books and more books. He was studying to be a lawyer, so he wanted books for Christmas, birthdays, and any other gift-giving times. Jana felt that books were unromantic and boring. The fun of planning to surprise Keith was taken out of gift-buying when she had to shop from his list of desired books. Gifts became an issue in their relationship until Jana decided that, since she couldn't change her husband, she would adopt his goals. She watched the ads in journals, attended estate sales, and sent away for discount book catalogs so that she could buy the desired books at a bargain. Keith was amazed at her success. At one estate sale (a former judge's) she was able to buy 51 books from his list. Within a few months, the law library had changed from a problem to a mutual project.

The prophet Amos had something important to say about relationships (Amos 3:3). He said that two people couldn't walk together until they agreed. There cannot be harmony if one person is trying to go in one direction and the other person is straining in the opposite direction. Couples need mutual goals on which they can work.

3. Were you able to be open in your communications? Could you tell each other what you were thinking and feeling? Could you communicate your anger even while confirming your love for one another? Perhaps you need to learn to be more open about your feelings. Perhaps you need to improve your listening skills.

James reminds us that it is important in relationships to be quick to listen and slow to speak (James 1:19). Remember how special you feel when someone pays attention to what you are saying or gives serious consideration to your ideas? Learn to give the gift of listening to your partner.

4. Were you accepting and affirming? A strong relationship develops when people accept and affirm one another—when they are proud and excited for one another's achievements. How do you rate in this area? Were you critical in public as well as in private? Did you belittle your partner? Did you jump in to rescue your partner, implying that he/she was incapable of handling situations alone? Did you find it hard to compliment your spouse? Perhaps you need to practice new behaviors in this area.

James wrote that the tongue causes serious problems unless a person maintains control over what is said (James 3:5–18). More important, Jesus said that our words are a reflection of our hearts (Luke 6:45). If we want to control our tongues, we must begin by changing our hearts. A person who is bitter inside will inevitably speak bitterly, but a person who is gentle and kind inside will speak gently.

5. Were you assertive and responsible for yourself? Did you depend upon a spouse to take care of you to the extent that you became a burden? Did you expect your spouse to be a mind reader and know what you were thinking or wanting?

Dean grew up in a family where a person always had to do what was expected of him. Illness was the only excuse for not doing so. During his marriage he was frequently sick on weekends. He could work all week, but he would wake up on Saturday mornings with a severe headache or a stomachache. He never realized that his body was simply cooperating with him. Each weekend his wife had a long list of things she wanted him to do. When the list was too long or included something Dean particularly hated doing, he would be sick. (Our bodies are marvelous. If we "need" to be sick, we will be!) Being sick was Dean's way of getting out of disagreeable chores.

When Dean was divorced, he found that he wasn't sick on weekends any more. When a friend pointed this out, Dean took a look at his history and realized that he needed to learn to express himself verbally and to arrange for having things done if he truly hated doing them himself.

In what areas were you less than assertive? In what areas do you need to take responsibility for yourself?

In his letter to the church at Thessalonica, Paul reminded the congregation that it was important for each person to pull his/her own weight (2 Thess. 3:6–14). Paul even went so far as to say that if a person didn't work, he shouldn't eat! One application for us is that we should not depend on others to take care of us or to rescue us. We must do our own work and take responsibility for our own lives.

6. Were you open to constructive criticism? It's hard to be criticized, particularly by someone you want to love and appreciate you. Now that you are out of a relationship, consider the criticism you may have received over the years and evaluate the validity of those comments. Is there something about your eating habits that annoys people? Do you repeat the same stories and jokes ad nauseam? Do you need to become more thoughtful of others? Are you too frugal or too generous? List the criticisms you can remember and consider each one. This is a time to grow. We are expected, as members of the body of Christ, to speak the truth in love one to another (Eph. 4:15). Sometimes difficult to hear, loving truth is often necessary for our growth.

7. Were your priorities right? *Leonard worked hard. He went to work early and stayed late, trying to get ahead and earn a good living for his family. He missed his wife's birthday dinner, his daughter's play, and his son's Little League games. He was working during parent-teacher conferences, school parties, and the annual Fourth of July parade in his town. He was too busy for playing ball in the backyard, taking out the trash, or going out to dinner. His boss loved him and promoted him. His wife loved him and left him.*

Now is the time to study your priorities and if, in fact, you have time for a relationship just now. You will not want to begin a new relationship or consider marriage until you have the necessary time to develop and maintain that relationship. As important as a career is, one's family must have significant priority if it is to survive.

Paul wrote strong words to Timothy about people taking care of their own families. This applies to providing the basic necessities of food and shelter and to providing the love, attention, affirmation, and respect that family members need. (See 1 Tim. 5:8.)

8. Were you financially responsible? Were you part of the problem or part of the solution? Did you spend money you didn't have or were you the one who worked overtime to pay the extra bills? In a marriage, both parties must share similar financial goals, or money will become one of the biggest problems.

For Loretta, spending money was her way of coping with problems. When she was depressed, she bought something. When she was angry, she grabbed her charge card and headed for the store. When she was having problems with her boss, she bought a new dress. Spending money was how she rewarded herself. Spending money was how she punished her husband. Spending money was how she showed her children that she loved them. When her husband had had enough, he left. Loretta needs to get rid of her unhealthy attitudes toward spending money.

Every good and perfect gift comes from God (James 1:17). This includes our careers and our paychecks. We are responsible to Him for how we receive and how we use what He gives. To use our money inappropriately is a sign of immaturity and ungratefulness for God's provision for us.

9. Were you loving? Did you assume that your spouse knew that you loved him/her? Or were you able to express your love in words, with cards, flowers, special meals, and affectionate touches? Perhaps you need to learn how to be more open in expressing your love and affection.

John tells us that we are to show our love not just in words but also by our actions (1 John 3:18). Words without accompanying actions are often meaningless.

Consider your former marriage as a mirror into which you look to see how you will function in a new relationship. If you see things you don't like, then take the time to make changes that will make you a better partner. If you feel that you did most things well and that you contributed to the building of the marriage rather than to the destruction of it, that is good. But each of us has weaknesses, and it is helpful to acknowledge them and work to change them into strengths.

Seek God's help. He has been with you during the tough times as you dealt with the loss of your marriage. Now ask Him to help you move on, to make positive changes so you can be more of what He wants you to be. Ask for strength, insight, confidence, encouragement, and affirmation as you try to bring about constructive change in your life.

Don't Be Afraid

Peggy has been divorced five years and hasn't had a date. She is scared. Although she is lonely, she is more afraid of being rejected again than of being alone for the rest of her life.

Peggy is so sensitive to rejection that she often perceives rejection where there is none. If someone disagrees with her opinion or doesn't share her preference in food, she takes this personally and feels rejected. If there isn't instant acceptance and approval, Peggy assumes rejection. Peggy has a big problem.

People who fear rejection may discover they have developed behaviors that they hope will prevent rejection. However, these very behaviors often create rejection. Such behaviors may include

- being closed in relationships, shutting people out;

- rejecting others before they can reject you;
- becoming egocentric, giving the message that you don't need anyone else's approval;
- putting yourself down, rejecting yourself before someone else can;
- becoming a people pleaser.

A people pleaser puts up with anything in a relationship for the sake of not losing the relationship. A people pleaser so desperately needs approval that he/she will give anything, do anything, or become anything that the other person wants them to be. In the process the people pleaser loses himself/herself and becomes a phoney person who ends up being rejected. A good resource if you are having problems because you are a people pleaser is my book *Pleasing You Is Destroying Me* (Word, 1992).

Instead of fearing rejection, acknowledge that everyone experiences rejection at some level. You have been rejected before, and you, or your ideas, will be rejected again. But you have survived rejection and will be able to survive it again. Be aware that you can set yourself up for being rejected by not developing good relational skills or not learning from your past experiences. Sometimes what we experience as a personal rejection is not really all that personal!

You have invited Glenn to go out after singles group for pie and coffee several times and he always says no. It may feel as if he doesn't want to go out with you specifically. However, Glenn has a serious weight problem, and he is working hard on his diet. He knows that late night snacks are his weakness and that pie is a particular favorite. Instead of tempting his diet, Glenn avoids restaurants after supper. His no is not personal.

It may happen that a person isn't ready for any relationship. The "rejection" of your overtures is not genuinely personal. That person would "reject" overtures from anyone at this time in his/her life. Learn to separate real rejection from perceived or felt rejection.

When you are ready, risk reaching out. Don't be afraid of not connecting the first time out.

Geoff is afraid of failing a second time. He has become almost commitment-phobic. He wants a guarantee that he will never be divorced again. He believes that he can't live through another divorce. His fears are so exaggerated that he won't have more than two dates with any woman. Until someone gives him a guarantee, he won't make another commitment. Geoff may never remarry, which is okay, except that Geoff desperately wants to be married and has not accepted his single-adult status.

I can identify with Geoff. I wanted a guarantee that a new relationship would last before I would marry a second time. I had to face the reality that only God knew the future and even if a man promised me forever there was no way to know that he would stay. It was a scary decision, but I am glad I made it because my relationship with my husband is wonderful.

Before you even think of remarriage, realize that you have been rescued from fear. You are not called to be in bondage to fear in your life. (See Rom. 8:12–15.) God has made provisions so you need not live in fear. Choose to let go of your fears.

One way to overcome your fears is to prepare for the possibility that you may remarry one day. Visit a Bible bookstore and get copies of several books on remarriage. If you have children, or the person you marry has children, you will become part of a stepfamily. You might want to read my book *Merging Families* (Concordia, 1992).

You Don't Have to Marry Again

Liz has been single for several years, has dated several men and has lots of friends of both sexes. Liz isn't sure she ever wants to get married again. That's terrific!

There may be different reasons you don't want to consider remarriage. Perhaps your religious beliefs do not allow for a second marriage after a divorce. Perhaps you have decided to pursue a personal goal that is not compatible with marriage. Perhaps you have developed a personal lifestyle that is comfortable and happy and does not include marriage. That's terrific!

No one says you must be married to be whole. You don't need to be married to be happy and joyful. Marriage is not required for a full life. Marriage is not the goal, wholeness is.

Right now, you are single. Make the most of this time in your life. Accept the present and use this time for personal and spiritual growth. Make your life into what God would have for you. Develop your spiritual gifts and get involved in ministry. Develop lots of healthy relationships with both men and women. If you happen to meet someone who is good for you, and you are good for that person, then concentrate on developing a wonderful relationship. Go ahead, fall in love again.

Affirmation of Peace

"I have peace in my life because God is in charge of my relationships and the direction of my life. I feel content with my life as it is today." Repeat this affirmation several times a day. It is based on the following Scripture verses:

Phil. 4:7 "And the peace of God, which transcends all understanding, will guard your hearts and your minds in Christ Jesus."

Phil. 4:12–13: "I know what it is to be in need, and I know what it is to have plenty. I have learned the secret of being content in any and every situation, whether well fed or hungry, whether living in plenty or in want. I can do everything through Him who gives me strength."

Reflections

- What is your first response to the idea that you might fall in love again?

- What would cause you to rush into a new relationship?
- What would be a realistic assessment of your relationship with your spouse during your former marriage?
- What weaknesses or problems in your former relationship will you work to avoid in future relationships?
- What relational skills do you feel you need to work on?
- What are your fears about getting into a new relationship?
- What is your response to the idea of remaining single for the next few years . . . for the rest of your life?
- Describe your idea of a good marriage.
- In what ways do you make yourself available to meet members of the opposite sex?
- What are you doing to become a good marriage partner should you ever remarry?

Relationship Preparation Activities

Check off the following activities as you complete each one.

- [ ] 1. Critique your relationship with your former spouse.
- [ ] 2. List the friends you had in your marriage. Evaluate your relationship with them and with your spouse and the expectations you had for both.
- [ ] 3. List the goals you shared in your marriage.
- [ ] 4. List the goals you and your spouse had that were counterproductive to the relationship.
- [ ] 5. Identify ways you can improve your skills in expressing love and affection to a spouse or dating partner.
- [ ] 6. Identify ways in which you failed to take responsibility for yourself and your life during your marriage.

- [ ] 7. List criticisms you have received in the past and evaluate each one for validity.
- [ ] 8. Identify the priorities you held during your marriage and evaluate how they may have affected the relationship.
- [ ] 9. List your attitudes about spending money and identify any problems you need to work on.
- [ ] 10. Get input and advice from a trusted friend on your personal assessments.
- [ ] 11. Plan how to begin making improvements in your relational skills.

11

"I'm Still a Sexual Being"

"My biggest problem right now seems to be how to handle my sexuality," Chet confessed at his small group meeting one night. "I was married for 22 years and had an active, satisfying sexual relationship with my wife. It's difficult to be suddenly celibate."

The group was discussing how Christian single adults needed to deal with their sexuality. Several group members spoke up.

"I know what you mean," Joyce agreed. "I miss the intimacy of being held and cuddled and making love. Sometimes I wonder if I am still alive because I go for weeks without ever being touched by another adult."

"Yeah! Me too!" Mark laughed ruefully. "I'm not ready to get married again, but I sure am ready for sex!"

"It's a different world out there from when I was single as a teenager," Ellen commented. "The big question then was whether to kiss on the first date. Today the question is frequently whether I will be expected to go to bed with a guy on the first date. I get the feeling that if I don't, there is something wrong with me!"

Is Everyone Doing It?

According to popular magazines, most single adults are—or will be—involved in a sexual relationship. However, one must ask if the surveys included active Christian, single adults. There is no question that even Christian single adults are sexually involved, regardless of their personal convictions or what God says about celibacy until marriage.

People become sexually active for a variety of reasons, many of which are not about physical release or satisfaction. There are several *excuses* people use for becoming involved:

1. "I'm scared to be alone." *Velma had never been alone. She went from her parents' home to her married home and, until her divorce at 43, had never spent a night alone. She was so scared of being alone that she got involved in a relationship with a man she didn't love, just so someone would be with her at night.*

Velma can remember that in the night hours, God never slumbers nor sleeps (Ps. 121:1–8) and that He will protect her.

2. "I don't want to lose this relationship." *Claudia said no to sex with three different men, all of whom quit dating her. When she met Patrick, she didn't want to lose him, so she said yes. In her heart, Claudia felt guilty, but her fear of being without a dating partner was greater than her guilt.*

Claudia forgets that any relationship is not right for her if it stands between her and obedience to God's Word. God still loves her, but their fellowship is impaired by her deliberate disobedience.

3. "I need to know that I am still desirable." Single adults whose spouses have left them often need to feel they are still desirable to the opposite sex, so they respond to sexual overtures. These people substitute sex for positive self-esteem, becoming involved in a series of relationships.

A healthier approach is to acknowledge the good feeling

of being desired by the opposite sex and understanding that in an appropriate relationship—marriage—sex is a great affirmation of that attraction. However, one's self-esteem does not depend on being desired by someone else.

4. "It helps to stop the pain." *Jack says that when he has sex he can temporarily forget the pain of his divorce and rejection. "It's only for a few hours, but it feels so good not to hurt!"*

Some single adults find that sex is a kind of anesthesia for the emotional pain. But no one can say that sex "cures" or eliminates the pain! Using sex as an anesthesia is like taking pain pills for a broken leg without having a doctor set the leg. As soon as the effect of the pill wears off, the pain returns. The bone may heal, but if it heals improperly, pain will continue.

The emotional pain of rejection, divorce, or loneliness must be treated and healed properly, not anesthetized with sex. The Christ who gives us strength in all things will help us join with Moses in choosing to be obedient—even when it's difficult—rather than enjoying the temporary pleasures of sin (Heb. 11:25). Jesus suffered every painful feeling we experience. God will not let you be tempted beyond what you can bear (1 Cor. 10:13).

5. "It makes me feel powerful." *"When I have sex with my partner and satisfy her, I feel powerful, strong, and capable."* Gary admits. *"Right now I feel that in most areas of my life I am powerless, a victim, incapable of doing things right, and a failure. I don't like that feeling."*

Some people see sex as a conquest in which the victor is the one who gets an attractive partner to say yes. Some are sexual scalp hunters, proud of the numbers. These people have failed to recognize that God created us as sexual human beings within a certain context. To misuse our bodies in a sexual way is destructive to both partners. God holds our bodies in high regard. Thanks to Jesus' death and resurrection, our bodies are destined for resurrection as well (1 Cor. 6:14).

6. "I'm addicted. I can't help myself." I've heard a few single adults state that they are addicted to sex and can't give it up. Sexual addiction can be as devastating as any other addictive behavior. But God can help the person confront the addiction and the issues behind the addiction, and make the necessary life changes.

When we are addicted to anything, we are no longer in control of our own lives. We are living for the addiction. Paul states, "Do you not know that your body is a temple of the Holy Spirit, who is in you, whom you have received from God? You are not your own; you were bought at a price. Therefore honor God with your body" (1 Cor. 6:19–20). We value our bodies as sacred places where God dwells. His Spirit's presence and power help us against such sins as sexual immorality and addictions.

7. "I don't know what else to do in a relationship." *Oscar explained his problem: "I guess I grew up unaware of the dynamics of relationships between men and women. Basically I thought that women were for having sex and kids with. I never thought about working on a relationship from an emotional or intellectual approach. So, here I am, going out with women, and I don't know what else to do with them except get involved sexually. I need to do something different! Where do I start?"*

There are single adults who never learned how to develop intimacy in any way except the physical. They need to learn how to relate on an intellectual level—sharing ideas, dreams, fears, experiences, and opinions. They need to learn to relate on an emotional level—giving support, caring, bearing another's burdens, and affirming another's personal and spiritual growth. They can relate recreationally as they play together—sports, activities, games, walking on the beach, picnicking in the park, or watching a movie. They can develop a partnership as they work together on projects—painting the house, cleaning the garage, making a garden, volunteering at the nursing home, or helping other single adults. They can develop the spiritual dimension of relationships as they share their personal journeys, as they pray together, study the Word, or take a class at church. There are many facets to successful relationships. People who want wholesome and healthy relationships will develop skills in these important areas.

Our relationships with others reflect our relationship with the Lord. Paul says in Eph. 2:1–10 that we have been saved from sin and lifted up to a heavenly status in Christ Jesus. We are His workmanship, created in Christ Jesus to do *good* works.

8. "Being good didn't work, so who cares what I do?" *Milly was a virgin when she married. She was a faithful wife for 10 years and always tried to live up to the standards presented in God's Word. When her husband left her, she felt let down and angry because "being good didn't work" and for a short period she "made up for lost time" with no regard for right or wrong.*

Soon she realized that although she was angry with her ex-husband—and even at God—for allowing this bad thing to happen to her, she was not resolving the situation by sinning. She acknowledged that she needed to deal with her anger and her desire for revenge. Once she did that, she recommitted her sexuality to the Lord. She lived in the freedom Christ died and rose to win her—the freedom to love and follow Him.

9. "It's my life and I'm not hurting anyone." *Ken's excuse is that his life is his own, and he isn't hurting anyone because he only has sex with willing partners. But Ken is way off base.*

Paul reminds us in 1 Cor. 6:19–20 that we have been bought with the blood of Christ. Our lives are God's.

Even if we have sex with a willing partner, we hurt that person by encouraging and assisting him/her in breaking God's law. By our actions, we disrupt that person's fellowship with God.

Even if a partner is interested and willing to have sex with us, we may encourage him/her to remain obedient if we do not give in to the temptation ourselves.

10. "I don't plan to have sex—it just happens." *Carol says that she never plans to have sex with a date. In fact, she tells herself before each date that she won't end up in bed this time. Yet often she does. Carol says she doesn't know how it happens, it just does.*

No, Carol, it doesn't.

Before you got into bed, you made a series of small decisions or agreements that led to the circumstance. For example, Carol, the sequence proceeded like this:

- You decided to accept the invitation for a date.
- You decided to stay in rather than to go out with a group or to a public place.
- You decided to turn the lights down to a more romantic level.
- You decided to sit close together on the couch.
- You decided to listen to romantic music.
- You decided to cuddle.
- You decided to begin touching each other suggestively.
- You decided to press your bodies together.
- You decided to partially undress.
- You decided to move to the bedroom to be more comfortable.
- You decided to undress.
- You decided to get into bed.
- You decided to have intercourse.

Whether Carol was the initiator or the responder, whether her decision was to start, or just to go along with her partner, she made the decisions. At any point she could have said no.

Of course, saying no is easier early in the sequence than later. Every single adult has to make decisions if he/she wants to be in control of his/her sexuality.

Take a stand as Joshua did and commit to following God and His principles for your life (Joshua 24:15).

11. "In our case, it's okay." *Emily presents a convoluted argument. She says that she and her former husband see each other socially, and that sometimes they have sex. "But," she argues, "in our case it is okay because we used to be married and that's different from having sex with a new partner."*

No, Emily, it isn't.

When the marriage relationship is dissolved, physical intimacy is no longer appropriate. It is just as wrong to have sex with your former spouse as it is to have sex with a new partner.

Roger and Gail are both divorced and are now engaged to be married to one another. Because they both want to get out of debt before they marry, their wedding date is eight months away. They don't see anything wrong with having sex because "we are going to get married, so what's the difference?"

The Word of God doesn't make exceptions for engaged couples or couples who were formerly married. God sets the same standard—celibacy—for all single adults (1 Cor. 6:9–11).

12. "I have unique needs, I have a strong sex drive." It is true that some people have a stronger need for sexual fulfillment, but this does not exclude them from God's standards. In fact, these people can claim the promise in 1 Cor. 10:13 that God is faithful and will provide a way to stand up to each temptation.

Assess Your Choices

Whatever your excuse to become involved sexually, it is time to make the right choice and confess your failings to God, seek His forgiveness, and promise Him that you will honor Him with your body and your life. The wonder of His grace is that each time we confess to Him and repent, we are forgiven—reinstated to close fellowship and renewed in our relationship to Him.

Take a few minutes to assess your own choices about your sexuality. If you have been tempted sexually, what excuses justified your giving in? Write those excuses on a sheet of paper. Next, do a Scripture search to see what God's response would be to each of your excuses. Keep this paper for easy reference the next time you toy with the idea of becoming involved sexually.

I am comforted by Paul's confession in Romans 7 that he sometimes doesn't do what he knows to be right and that other times he does what he knows to be wrong. But Rom. 8:1 reminds us that "there is now no condemnation for those who are in Christ Jesus . . . " We can look to Jesus as the one who enables us to walk rightly again. What a great God we serve!

What Are the Standards?

Sexuality is a fact of life. We were created as sexual human beings. And when God looked at all that He had created, He said that "it was very good" (Gen. 1:31). Sex is not bad or dirty. It is a beautiful gift that God gives us for use in a specific context—marriage.

Whether we are married or single, we have sexual desires and needs. God could have created us differently so that unless we were married, we wouldn't think about or want to have sex. But He didn't. He gave us our sexuality and then told us how to use it for the purposes for which it was designed. God gave sex for two purposes: to unite a husband and wife in special intimacy and to produce children. Sex in other contexts violates God's standards. (See 1 Cor. 6:9–20; Matt. 5:27–28; Eph. 5:3–12; 2 Peter 2:9–16.)

If sex is a strong temptation to you, do an exhaustive Bible study of sexual sin. Read the Bible stories of people who became sexually involved outside of marriage and list the consequences of their sin. Copy Bible verses that give God's standards for us in this area. This project can strengthen your commitment to abstinence.

In defining our sexuality, God gave us the standards of celibacy outside of marriage and faithfulness within marriage because He knows that is how we can best enjoy His gift to us.

Imagine unwrapping a new recording of a beautiful symphony and smashing it into a hundred pieces. Designed to produce many years of enjoyment, that recording will never be the same again. You could glue it together and try playing it on the stereo, but the music would be flawed and no longer enjoyable.

The same is true of your sexuality. If you misuse it, you will forfeit God's best for you. If you use it as designed, you will have a lifetime of fulfillment and enjoyment. But the simple fact is that you can't do it alone.

No matter how hard you try, *by yourself* you're not going to be able to use your sexuality in a God-pleasing way. All our striving to recover from divorce and build new relationships requires His strength to supplement our own.

Look to Jesus Christ as your Savior. He paid for your sins of misused sexuality, of broken relationships, of sinful desires—and everything else. Through His death on the cross, He took your sins away from you and carried them Himself. Not only did He pay for your sins, He conquered them by rising from the dead. Because He lives, there is a renewed relationship between you and God.

And that is the message of the Gospel. God wants *the best* for us. Through Jesus Christ, He wants us to know the fulfillment of the abundant life (John 10:10). He wants us to know the joy of living in His will as we present our bodies to Him as a living sacrifice (Rom. 12:1–2). He wants us to have His joy, and for our joy to be full as, through the power of the Holy Spirit, we abide in Him and keep His commandments (John 15:10–11). And the things that God has prepared for us are beyond our knowledge, our dreams, and our imaginations (1 Cor. 2:9). The thoughts and plans He has for us are good, not evil, because in Christ He gives us a future and a hope (Jer. 29:11).

God's best includes a long list of things which give us happiness when we use His gift of sex in the right context:

Sex in Marriage, God's Design, Can Bring	Sex Outside of Marriage Can Cause
Peace of mind	Anxiety
Completeness	Incompleteness
Nurturing relationships	Destructive relationships
Wholeness	Brokenness as relationships dissolve
Physical, emotional, and spiritual health	Physical, emotional, and spiritual distress
Joy	Sadness
True intimacy	False intimacy
Love	Rejection
Fulfillment	Dissatisfaction
Pleasure	Disillusionment
Partnership	Self-Centeredness or being taken advantage of
Fellowship with Him	Loss of fellowship with God

Make the Right Choice

As you rebuild your life after a devastating experience, make good choices. Don't let yourself give into the temptation to become sexually active or to excuse away your behavior. Seek God's help and strength to build a life that pleases Him. That joy is only available to us as we trust in Jesus as our Savior and Lord. You might want to read *Too Close, Too Soon* by Jim Talley and Bobbie Reed (Thomas Nelson, 1982).

1. Decide to be celibate. The first step is to decide to be celibate. Don't wait until you are confronted with the situation before you make your choice. Because you want the best in your life, pray for God's help and guidance.

2. Communicate your decision. You don't have to wear a button that says "I will not have sex!" However, if you are in a dating relationship, it is appropriate and helpful to openly discuss sex and your decision that you will not have sex outside of marriage.

3. Plan safe dates. Don't plan or agree to dates that will be sexually tempting. Instead, go out together to public places. Get involved in activities, especially with other people. Work on projects together. Work at building emotional, recreational, spiritual, and intellectual intimacy while placing the physical on hold. Limit the time you spend alone to short periods and few dates. Don't go to "sexy" movies. These things will reduce the temptations you face.

4. Control your thoughts. Don't give your mind a lot of sexual stimuli. Avoid sexual magazines or sexually explicit movies or novels. Don't spend time fantasizing about a sexual experience. Don't dwell on how much you wish you were sexually fulfilled.

Instead fill your mind with the Word of God. When I was given a new Bible for my 15th birthday, my mother wrote on the flyleaf: "Remember, this book will keep you from sin—or sin will keep you from this book." David knew the secret when he wrote that he hid the Word of God in his heart so that he would not sin against God (Ps. 119:11).

Your personal devotions and prayer time are important

when you are engaged in a spiritual warfare. And in the sexual area, it is often a war between your flesh and Satan and you and God. Gird yourself for the fight (Eph. 6:11–18).

5. Share your struggles with God. As you pray, confess your struggles and temptations with the Lord and ask for His strength. Ask Him to give you insight to help you grow in the area of relationships so that you can be a better friend or partner. Phil. 4:13 says that we can do anything through Christ who strengthens us. He can identify with our struggles and help us through them.

6. Get "legal" physical affirmation. An important element in an effective single-adult ministry is warm "bear" hugs. We need to be physically affirmed. Smiles are nice. Handshakes are nice. But there is nothing like a warm hug from someone who cares about how you are doing.

You will want to have several people in your life to whom you can go and say, "I need a hug."

Some people find that they have an increased need for physical enjoyment during a time of celibacy. They go to a masseuse, sit in hot tubs, take warm baths, or have their children give them back rubs.

7. Develop a strong support group of friends. It is easier to be strong when you surround yourself with friends who will encourage you to make healthy choices. Sitting home alone and lonely will only add to your dissatisfaction with being single again. It will sap your strength to resist temptation.

Get involved in lots of activities. Plan your alone time well. Instead of standing at the closed door in your life and feeling sorry for yourself, enjoy all of the opportunities that are open to you. Make your life full and joyful.

Affirmation of Right Choices

"I am excitedly choosing to live according to God's standards because I want to experience His joy. I feel

pleased that I make good choices in my relationships."
Repeat this affirmation several times a day. It is based on the following verses from Scripture:

Titus 3:8: "This is a trustworthy saying. And I want you to stress these things, so that those who have trusted in God may be careful to devote themselves to doing what is good. These things are excellent and profitable for everyone."

John 15:9–11: "As the Father has loved me, so have I loved you. Now remain in my love. If you obey my commands, you will remain in my love, just as I have obeyed my Father's command and remain in His love. I have told you this so that my joy may be in you and that your joy may be complete."

Reflections

- What sexual temptations/challenges are most difficult for you to handle?
- What excuses for giving into temptation come to your mind when you are in a sexual situation?
- What sexually stimulating activities have you decided to eliminate from your life now that you are single again?
- What things have you discovered to help you resist sexual temptation?
- What physically satisfying and "legal" activities have you substituted for sexual gratification since you are single again?
- What verses of Scripture are helpful to you in sexual situations?
- What kinds of dates would be "safe" for you?
- What are your fears about choosing to remain celibate?
- What reasons would you give your teenager for his/her remaining celibate?
- How do you feel about entrusting your sexuality to God?
- How can you gather strength from God to handle your sexuality?

Positive Choice Activities

Check off each suggested step as you complete it.

- [ ] 1. Write your "excuse" for giving into sexual temptation.
- [ ] 2. Do a Scripture search of God's responses to each "excuse" you have written.
- [ ] 3. Do an exhaustive Bible study on sexual sin and its consequences.
- [ ] 4. Confess your past sexual sins (including the sinful thoughts) to God, ask His forgiveness because of Jesus Christ, and call on Him to give you strength to deal with your sexuality.
- [ ] 5. Decide to be celibate.
- [ ] 6. Communicate your decision to a dating partner.
- [ ] 7. Plan safe dates.
- [ ] 8. Control your thoughts.
- [ ] 9. Share your struggles with God.
- [ ] 10. Get "legal" physical affirmation.
- [ ] 11. Develop a strong support group of friends.

12

"I Need My Friends"

"It was strange." Sharon shares. "I woke up one morning and suddenly I had this overwhelming urge to get on with my life. I wanted to make new friends and try out different activities. It was time to get on with the business of starting over."

Tom agreed. *"I had a similar experience. I was sitting on my patio one evening, and I realized that my life had been on hold while I was getting through the mourning process for my marriage. I felt as if I were being awakened from an emotional sleep and was ready to reach out again. I wanted to reconnect with my old friends and find new ones."*

Whether your desire to reach out is to build new friendships or to restructure existing relationships, you really do need your friends. Where do you start?

Let People Know You Are Available

During your grieving period, you probably were unable to give much to the relationships and friendships in your life. Most likely, you were too busy trying to cope with staying alive, keeping your job, maintaining your home, and caring for your children or pets. Now you have more energy and interest in including others in your life. It's time to review your list of friends.

Some people in your life have stood by you, even if you

were not receptive to their caring. They remembered you daily in prayer. These friends will be glad to see you take an interest in life again. They will notice when your protective shield begins to fade. They will be ready with invitations and ideas for how you might spend your time. Call these people first. Be prepared for a bit of gentle teasing. Admit that you are a bit tentative, but that you are ready to get involved in life again.

The next group to contact are those casual friends with whom you did specific activities (football tailgating, beach parties, strawberry picking). Get on the telephone and ask them to include you in the next event or activity. Explain that you have been through a difficult time and are going to need their help in reconnecting, and even in meeting new friends of both sexes. You don't need to go into details about your divorce, although you may need to make them aware of it. Be willing to participate in some activities that may not sound interesting, just in order to meet new people in new surroundings.

Consider the people in your classes, church, organizations, or workplace. Are there some you would like to know better? Ask them, one at a time, for a cup of coffee and get acquainted. Ask them about interesting things to do on weekends. You will get several invitations this way. Follow up on the invitations and you will meet new people.

Volunteer to have the next Sunday school class or single-adult group party at your house. You will have a chance to meet new people, as it will be your role as host to greet them and make them comfortable. Even shy people can reach new people by having a party. Each week, do something to ensure that you meet new people.

When rebuilding your friendship support system, it is important that you risk doing new things. Don't fall back into the same rut as before, however comfortable it may have been. There is a time for most things in life (Eccl. 3:1–8). This is a time for new and different adventures.

Assess Your Friendship Support System

Brad has three intimate friends with whom he does everything. He can be open and honest with these friends, sharing his feelings and secrets. But Brad doesn't have much to do with other people. He is either with one or more of his three friends, or he is alone, or at work.

Kathy has lots of casual friends. Everywhere she goes people wave at and greet her. She seems to always be smiling and never "down." Kathy is fun to be around and, in a group, is usually the center of attention. She is witty and interesting. But Kathy never tells anyone about her depression, her fears, her anger, or her private dreams. Kathy is rarely alone, or with only one friend. She is usually in a crowd.

Stan has found a balance. He has a couple of intimate friends, several close friends, and lots of casual friends.

Most of us need three types of friendships to function well. We need intimate, close, and casual friends.

Have you kept a balance in your social support system during this time of recovery and rebuilding? If you have, congratulations! If you, like most people, have let some relationships slide, it is time to take stock and assess your personal support system and see where it needs attention.

1. You need intimate friends. Intimate friends are those *four to seven* people whose emotional support and depth of involvement with you are strong. These friends are readily available to you. They accept you where you are, affirm you, and have frequent contact with you.

Write the names of those you consider to be your intimate friends. Note the last time you spent time with each one. Check out your emotional response to each one as you write the name. Do you still feel comfortable sharing with that person about your inner self? Does this person still share with you, or has he/she withdrawn a bit since your divorce? If there has been a withdrawal could it have been because of your own withdrawal? Is this still someone you want to have as your intimate friend?

2. You need close friends. Close friends are those *15–20* people who are important in your life and whom you see regularly. These people are aware and care about you even if you don't share intimately with them. They provide companionship, enrichment, entertainment, and diversion. Close friends are often project- or activity- specific.

Now write the names of people whom you consider to be close friends. Again, note the last time you spent time with each one. Jot down what triggered the contact. Mentally review each person on you list. Is this a person you still want to include as a close friend? How do you think that person feels about you? How can you initiate contact in the next week? Is there someone you would like to have as a new close friend? What could you do to start on that relationship?

3. You need casual friends. Casual friends are those *30–50* people who have some intermittent contact with you, but are not what you consider close friends. These people are in the outer circle of your social group, but provide resources (tickets to games, information about job opportunities) and stimulation in your life (physical, spiritual, or mental). They may be members of your single-adult group, a collection of coworkers, or members of a club to which you belong.

List several people you consider to be casual friends. Think of ways to increase your list, if it is short. What activities would help you meet new people to add to your list of casual friends?

Each type of friend is important in your life. Consider the example we see in the life of Jesus while He was here on earth. He had a lot of acquaintances, who followed Him around waiting to hear Him speak or see Him perform miracles. He also had casual friends. Perhaps it was one of those at whose wedding He turned the water into wine. He had 12 close friends He called His disciples. But even from within this group, He had three intimate friends: Peter, James and John. (See Matt. 17:1–13 and 26:36–46.)

It is best if there is a mix of people in each group: single adults, married people, older and younger people, and both men and women. Each friendship requires time and energy to develop and maintain, as friendships are dynamic, not static. They are always changing.

Friendships change as people change. People move in the friendship levels as the priorities and circumstances in their lives change. You need to be prepared for such changes. Learn to build long-term, solid friendships, but be open to enjoying short-term friendships for what they can offer.

If you find that your social support system is not balanced, that you have too many or too few friends in one category, or all women or all men friends, all single or all married friends, work on restructuring your friendships.

Restructure Your Support System

This is an important time in your life. You need a very strong friendship foundation upon which to rebuild your new life. Take time to ensure that this is in place.

1. Release nonproductive relationships. *Shelly had a habit of clinging to friendships, even when they were no longer productive. She wrote long, personal letters to old schoolmates who never wrote back. She baked cookies and made fudge to take to work at least once a week. People stopped by for the treats, but rarely stayed long enough to say hi, let alone to visit. When she assessed her friendships, Shelley admitted she spent a great deal of energy maintaining one-sided relationships.*

She decided to divert some of that energy into developing two-way friendships. She put the schoolmates on her Christmas card list instead of her personal letter list. She brought snacks to the singles group at church, where people visited before class began. Almost immediately, she felt rewarded as she met new friends at church.

Maybe you have held on too long to some nonproductive relationships. You don't have to cut them out of your life totally. If the relationship is not contributing to your life, or is not helpful to the other person, maybe it is time to invest less energy in that relationship.

2. Concentrate on good relationships. *Russ decided to concentrate on several good friendships. He evaluated each intimate friendship and several close friendships. One man, a close friend, had been extremely supportive during his divorce. Before that time, Russ had never shared on a personal level with this man. Now, he realized that this person belonged in his intimate friendship circle.*

You may want to make room in your intimate circle for additional friends. Contact those people and share your desires to move your relationship to a different level. If both of you are interested in doing this, you will be successful. Move a casual friendship to a close one by spending more time together—talking, sharing, working on a project, or doing activities of interest to both of you. Risk being more open about your feelings. Share who you are and where you are in your personal journey. Be willing to listen to the other person. Learn to care—really care— about what is happening in his/her life.

3. Find new people for your support system. *Lance decided that he didn't have a sufficiently large circle of casual friends. So, he outlined a plan of action. He went to interesting places, got involved in fun activities, and started conversations with strangers wherever he was. This wasn't easy, but he told himself it was a "homework exercise" that had to be done. He began enjoying himself as he overcame his shyness.*

"I couldn't believe what I did sometimes," Lance said. "Once I was standing in line waiting for tickets to a play. I asked the person behind me what he knew about the play.

The next thing I knew we were talking so excitedly that someone had to remind us to move forward in line!"

You can learn to reach out, even if it is difficult for you. If you see someone wearing an unusual pin, tie, or hat, or unusual jewelry, comment on it. Ask if it was made especially for him/her. Start a discussion about style and personal taste.

If you see someone carrying a book, ask how he/she likes what they are reading. (The key word is *carrying* a book; you might get rebuffed if you start talking to someone who is trying to *read* a book.) Ask if they have read other books by the same author. Volunteer information about your favorite authors, and see if you find any similarities in your reading tastes.

Take a chance. What can happen? Someone might turn away, but chances are very good that some people will talk with you—and that you will find each other interesting. If a conversation develops, suggest that you go for a cup of coffee, or a glass of iced tea, and get acquainted. A good resource for this step of getting your life in order is my book *Learn to Risk* (Zondervan, 1990).

Fine-tune Your Relational Skills

When Lance started reaching out in a new way, he discovered that he needed to work on his relational skills. In the past he hadn't concentrated on building friendships—they just happened to exist. He wasn't aware of what he was doing or not doing to encourage the relationships. Now he wanted to develop solid friendships and reach out to new people.

Perhaps you have some work to do in this area. If you had problems with developing and maintaining friendships in the past, focus on the following skills.

1. Excel at small talk. Most of the time I hate small talk. It seems so inane. I mean, who really cares about the weather, the news, the scenery, or bargains at the grocery store? I cherish conversations in which I sense a connection on an emotional level, a mental challenge, or a spiritual inspiration. I can get high on those conversations. But I rarely have those conversations at a first meeting!

Initiating conversations with strangers usually involves small talk. This means getting their attention without scaring them away. People have a zone of privacy, a psychological space, that must be entered if you are to reach them. Barging into that space too quickly usually results in their feeling invaded and you being rebuffed. Learn the art of discussing the inconsequential. Consider it an important step in opening new friendships. It's like the ritual of slowly taking the wrapping paper off a gift rather than ripping it off, tearing open the box, and possibly damaging the contents. "Unwrap" new friends slowly.

2. Risk self-disclosure. *Adele is a private person. She is a great friend if someone with infinite patience takes the time to cultivate her friendship. Not many people stay around long enough for Adele to feel comfortable sharing with them, so her friendships are few. Adele decided to risk self-disclosure.*

Vounteer information about yourself before you ask a question. Just asking questions may give the feeling of an "interview." When you are open about yourself, you invite the other person to be open, and there is a sense that this is a conversation.

You don't have to share your innermost secrets. Start with nonthreatening information. But give up something! Start a conversation with a person in a long line by admitting that you actually hate waiting in line. Confess your fantasy about forcing your way into the front of the line or about faking a disability so people will feel sorry and let you in line ahead of them— or whatever else goes through your mind. Then, as you laugh at your own silliness, ask the other person about his/her favorite "waiting in line" fantasy.

At a single adult function you might approach someone

standing apart and admit your own discomfort at being alone at a social gathering. If this is your first time, say so. Chances are the other person is experiencing some of the same feelings, and a conversation will begin.

3. Be a good conversationalist. It takes a certain amount of skill to keep a conversation going. There are things that make it easier. Avoid questions that can be answered with a yes or no. Don't ask someone if this is his/her first time at a singles event. You will have wasted a question, because after the yes or no, you will have to ask another question. Instead, ask what the person likes about the event, or how he/she heard about it, or what he/she thinks you can expect to happen. Or find some other question that invites more than a quick response.

A successful conversation is built on questions that invite sharing of feelings, ideas, fears, or hopes. Learn to phrase nonthreatening questions that encourage people to open up. It may take several questions before you actually get someone feeling comfortable enough to carry on a natural conversation. Keep trying.

Practice your listening skills. When you ask a question, be sure to listen to the response. This will give you clues for what to say next. Work at remembering what someone has told you about him/herself. A person feels special when someone remembers something from a previous conversation. You don't always have to be the one who is giving information. Learn to be an appreciative audience.

4. Be an assertive friend. *Shirley discovered that she had been basically a passive person for most of her life. She depended on others to look out for her interests, to draw her into conversations, and to fight her battles for her. When he left, her husband's parting shot was, "I'm tired of taking care of you! You had better learn to take care of yourself or no one will ever want to be around you!"*

"It was a rude awakening," Shirley admits. "But I started thinking about my life, and he was right. I really did need to learn to take care of myself."

Shirley did just that. It didn't happen overnight. Growing into an assertive person takes time and a lot of work, but Shirley declares that it is worth the effort.

Good friends are assertive. They take care of themselves so we don't have to. They "bear their own burdens" and pull their own weight in relationships (Gal. 6:2–5). They are open, honest and caring. They express their own opinions without dominating. They initiate contact with strangers as well as friends. When necessary they confront for the good of the relationship and accept confrontation and criticism as input to be considered. Assertive people give and accept compliments graciously; they ask for what they want (understanding that they won't always get it), and they are comfortable refusing unreasonable requests.

How do you measure up to that criteria? Are you an assertive friend—or are you still waiting to be rescued or taken care of? If there are areas in which you are not comfortable, set some goals and work on your relational skills.

Renewing Your Friendship with Your Ex

Roxanne is ready to reach out and to renew her friendship with her former spouse. She isn't interested in any romance or reconciliation. She just wants to be able to encounter him at social functions without her heart stopping or without awkward behavior. She wants to be able to call him about problems with the children without a sense of embarrassment and fear. You may be ready also.

At this point, you have moved past the pain and are building a whole new life for yourself, using parts of the old life as a foundation. There is a marvelous feeling of freedom as your thinking is clearer, your decision skills are sharper, and your emotions are stabilized. You have recovered your dignity, self-esteem, perspective, sense of balance, and security. Your fears are almost gone. Daily, you are affirming strength, faith, growth, thought-control, assertiveness, peace, forgiveness, joy, emotional control, positive self-image, and love in your life.

You have let go of the past. You are facing the future unafraid.

When you reach this place you probably still have one piece of unfinished business: reconnecting with your former spouse, renewing the friendship, and developing a workable relationship. Some people advocate a clean break, where the two parties have as little to do with one another as possible. This has value in the early days of grieving. However, it is not good to totally sever relationships.

1. Be clear about what you expect. Any breach in relationships within the body of Christ causes pain to the entire body. (See 1 Cor. 12:25–27.) Therefore, the body benefits when it is possible to reestablish a working relationship between former partners. When there are children, it is also important that both parents form a parenting coalition and continue to assist one another.

However, before you rush out and call him/her, be sure that you are ready.

Richard isn't ready. Each time he thinks about contacting Amy, his ex-wife, he gets sweaty palms, an upset stomach, and fantasizes about getting back together. Reconnecting is not about reviving a fantasy.

Estelle isn't ready either. Whenever she thinks about Marvin, she becomes angry and experiences again the pain that his leaving caused.

Wendy is ready. She has worked through her grief and her pain. She has accepted the reality that she and Larry are no longer married and won't ever be again. She has given up her anger and is no longer depressed about being single again.

Instead, she finds life a daily adventure, with some days being better than others. She has recognized that she and Larry used to be such good friends and that it would be a shame to throw away all of that relationship, particularly since they still have frequent contact because of their minor children. She has no illusions about the nature of the "new" friendship. It will not be the intimate relationship they once had. They probably won't be "best buddies." But she values his advice about the children and wants to remain friends.

You are ready when you can look forward to a cup of coffee and conversation with the same pleasant anticipation as you would if you were meeting any old friend. While there may be a few butterflies because the situation is unfamiliar, there won't be any panic or major emotional upheaval.

If you aren't ready, don't push it. You have the rest of your life to reconnect. Perhaps you are ready, but your former spouse isn't interested in maintaining any contact with you. Don't force it. In fact, reconnecting may never happen. The basic thing for you to be concerned about is your own attitude. If you are unwilling to meet, then you are probably not through the grieving process. You are still angry, depressed, hurt, or unsure of yourself. You haven't totally let go of the past and rebuilt your life.

Remember that we are to put aside all anger and malice and to relate to one another in a kind, tender, gentle manner (Eph. 4:29–32).

2. Prepare for the first meeting carefully. *"When I first thought about meeting Jason again, I was a nervous wreck!" Lucy admits. "Then I reminded myself that this wasn't a date."*

You're absolutely right, Lucy! Don't plan a meeting that will have any similarity to a date. Don't suggest that you go to "your restaurant" for a late dinner. Don't plan a suggestive, romantic evening at your house. Don't dress to entice, seduce, or prove what a good thing he/she has let go. Don't suggest meeting anywhere that has a special significance to you as a couple. Instead, select a neutral setting, have lunch or coffee and be open about what you want—a working relationship between the two of you.

Avoid topics that may be disruptive. This is not the time to discuss late support payments, problems with the children, dislike of your former spouse's new dating partner, or serious personal problems.

The first meeting needs to be short. If it doesn't go well, it will be over soon. If it does go well, you won't be tempted to fantasize about getting back together again.

Be prepared for some discomfort because this relationship will be unfamiliar to both of you. You may find that you only talk about inconsequential things. That's okay for the first meeting. The point is not to have a deep, significant conversation, but to open the door to a new style of friendship.

If your former spouse becomes amorous, don't give in to the temptation to respond in kind or to rebuff him/her. If you find yourself becoming sexually aroused during the encounter, don't take it seriously. You were married, after all, and have a sexual history with this person. It is not surprising that he/she can affect you in this way.

3. Build the new relationship carefully. Once you and your former spouse have reconnected and begun working at a new relationship, it is important to keep it in a proper perspective.

It isn't wise to get involved financially. Don't purchase property or make joint investments. You both have new lives that must remain separate one from the other.

It isn't wise to begin meeting several times a week. If you get together too often, one of you may get unrealistic expectations and end up getting hurt again. If both of you are serious about getting back together, then see a good Christian counselor and begin working on that process. Don't try to do it yourselves, because you will probably fail.

It isn't wise to become one another's confidant. You don't need to hear all about your former spouse's emotional involvement with other people, even if it makes you feel closer to him/her.

It isn't wise to depend on one another to assist with the practical things in your life. If you start taking care of one another again, your healing process will regress and you may find yourself in pain again.

Seek a healthy balance and become friends—when and if you are ready. Ready is when you can keep the relationship healthy for both of you.

Everyone needs friends. Be sure that your social support system is strong and that you have the friends you need to keep you going and growing.

Affirmation of Love

"I am a loving, giving, genuine person. I feel expectant about my future." Repeat this affirmation several times a day. It is based on the following passages from Scripture:

John 13:34–35: "A new command I give you: Love one another. As I have loved you, so you must love one another. By this all men will know that you are my disciples, if you love one another."

1 John 4:7: "Dear friends, let us love one another, for love comes from God. Everyone who loves has been born of God and knows God."

Reflections

- In what ways have you let (not let) people know you are available for friendship-building activities?

- Which friends have stood by you in very special and affirming ways?
- Which casual friends could you contact now that you are ready to work on friendships?
- Describe your friendship support system in terms of intimate, close, and casual friends.
- Which groups of people are not in your support system: married, single, older, younger, males, females?
- Why do you cling to relationships that are nonproductive?
- What are you doing now to improve the good relationships?
- What are you doing to add new people to your support system?
- Which relational skills do you need to work on?
- What is your response to the idea of renewing your friendship with your former spouse?

 Friendship Building Activities

Check off the following activities suggested in this chapter as you complete each one.

- [ ] 1. List your intimate friends and evaluate your relationship with each.
- [ ] 2. List your close friends and evaluate your relationships.
- [ ] 3. List several casual friends and evaluate your relationships.
- [ ] 4. Evaluate your social support system to ensure that it is balanced, full, and productive.
- [ ] 5. Let people know that you are available and interested in meeting new people of both sexes.

☐   6. Take responsibility for at least one activity each week in which you will meet new people.
☐   7. Release nonproductive relationships.
☐   8. Take steps to improve current friendships.
☐   9. Perfect your ability to engage in small talk.
☐ 10. Practice self-disclosure.
☐ 11. Risk self-disclosure in conversations with new people.
☐ 12. Improve your conversational skills.
☐ 13. Develop your assertive skills.
☐ 14. Decide if you are ready to reconnect with your former spouse.
☐ 15. Plan the meeting carefully.
☐ 16. Develop the new relationship carefully.
☐ 17. Use the affirmations daily.

Appendix
Developing a Divorce Recovery Support Group

Although people do recover from a divorce on their own, it is usually helpful for them to participate for several weeks in a divorce recovery support group. When people share their journeys in life, the healing seems to be faster. Group members encourage one another. They cry together. They support one another. They bond one with another. They even push one another to the tough decisions of rebuilding their lives.

Duration

The ideal length for a divorce recovery support group program is 12–14 weeks. However, it is difficult to get people to make a commitment for that long. Most churches or groups limit the program to 8 weeks. This book was designed to accommodate 8–12 weeks. The first 8 chapters follow the grieving cycle. All are necessary for recovery, so do not skip any chapters. The last 4 chapters focus on different aspects of rebuilding one's life after a divorce. These can be used for individual sessions, or participants can work through them on their own after the 8-week session is over.

Location

You can hold the support group meetings anywhere: church, home, community center, or school classroom. The important thing is that the sessions are located where you won't be interrupted. You will want to provide child care for parents.

Format

Before the sessions, provide a light snack (coffee, tea, punch, cookies, chips) for participants. Eating serves as a familiar activity that puts participants at ease. This time also allows for informal sharing between those who attend.

Each session should be 90 minutes to 2 hours long.

The first part of the session can be a *brief* personal sharing by a leader or a guest speaker who has successfully rebuilt his/her life after a divorce.

Next, schedule a 30 or 40-minute presentation of the content of the chapter for the week. The presenter may be the program coordinator, a guest speaker, or someone else who can share the material effectively.

Finally, divide the participants into small groups of 5–9 people for a discussion time. Use the "reflections" at the end of each chapter. Be aware that a group of 8 people can only address about 6 questions in an hour, so select the questions you want the group to focus on.

Leaders

One person should serve as overall coordinator for the divorce recovery support group program. You also will need a weekly presenter (who may be the coordinator, or another person, or several persons). And you will need one leader for each discussion group.

The person in charge of the divorce recovery support group program needs to have a deep empathy and understanding of what people go through in a divorce experience. While it is not required that the coordinator have personal experience, it is helpful to have some discussion leaders who have been through a divorce.

Discussion-group leaders are often people who have attended previous divorce recovery sessions and are further along in the recovery process. Being a small-group discussion leader is one way for people to speed up their personal healing. The leaders are responsible for ensuring that the guidelines are followed and for sharing on a personal basis. Their stories provide encouragement and hope for the current participants.

Discussion Guidelines

Before you divide into small groups each week, remind participants of the guidelines for the discussions. Here are several that work well:

- Everyone will be given an opportunity to share during the small-group discussion time.
- No one will be forced to participate in the discussion. However, the more people participate, the more they will get out of the session.
- Everyone is free to express his/her own opinion, but not to "preach," criticize, or change how someone else thinks. Keep comments in first person. Use "I statements," such as "I think . . ." or "I feel . . ."
- No one is allowed to belittle, mock, ridicule, or argue with something that is said during the discussion.
- Everyone will maintain confidentiality. Nothing that is said during the discussion time will be repeated later.
- No one will dominate the conversation. In order for everyone to have an opportunity to share, no one will respond to a question twice until everyone has a chance to respond once.

The function of the small-group leader is to maintain order in the group. If a person seems to want to share, but is shy, the leader will direct a question to that person. If someone is starting to "preach" or argue, the leader will intervene.

The plan for the small group discussion is to take one question and go around the circle allowing everyone to respond in turn, if they want to. In this way participants hear how others are feeling and responding to similar situations. They can gain confidence in realizing that "they aren't the only ones who feel that way."

Resources

For more information on developing a program for divorce recovery, try these resources:

- *Developing a Divorce Recovery Ministry* by Bill Flanagan (Navpress, 1991)
- *The Fresh Start Divorce Recovery Workbook* by Bob Burns and Tom Whiteman (Thomas Nelson, 1992)
- *The Complete Divorce Recovery Handbook* by John P. Splinter (Zondervan, 1992)
- *Growing through Divorce* by Jim Smoke (Harvest House, 1976)
- *Beginning Again* by Terry Hershey (Nelson, 1986)